ESSENTIAL EATS

An Essential Oil Cookbook©

Karen J. Ogden

ISBN: 978-1-781734-936704

www.essentialeatscookbook.com

Publisher's Note: The reader should not regard the recommendations, ideas and techniques expressed and described in this book as substitutes for the advice of a qualified medical practitioner or other qualified professional. Any use to which the recommendations, ideas, and techniques are put is at the reader's sole discretion and risk.

Dedication & Thanks: My mother, Jeanne, encouraged me to cook at an early age. She, too, was an avid home chef. Though she worked full time, she always put a delicious meal on the table every. She passed away in 2019, and I know she'd take great pride in that I am finishing my promise of a cookbook, and that I am dedicating it to her. Thanks, Mom, for all the great meal memories and for being one of my biggest cheerleaders.

As in all I do, my husband Scott is my biggest supporter. When I am convinced I can't, he reminds me that I can. My love and thanks to him.

Chef Martha Hubbard of Key West worked with me to proof these recipes. She also plated and photographed many of the dishes. Her encouragement, support, and friendship have been a source of motivation for me to finish what I started. Thank you, Martha.

Sources: Much of the information presented in *Essential Eats An Essential Oil Cookbook* was derived from a great number of resources and is seemingly public knowledge. However, there are two books that the author used on a regular basis in preparing this cookbook. They are listed below. The information contained within these books was verifiable among other sources, so there is no specific citing within the book. *Essential Oils Pocket Reference*, Sixth Edition, May 2014, by Life Science Publishing. *Rosemary Gladstar's Medicinal Herbs, A Beginner's Guide*, 2012, by Rosemary Gladstar, Storey Publishing,

Photography
Cover Photo by Karen J. Ogden
Martha Hubbard of Key West, Florida and Karen J. Ogden

Ceramic dishes and platters featured in many of the photographs were crafted by Mark Klammer of Shade Ceramics and Shutter Photography, Key West, Florida. A special thanks for letting me use them for this book. Please visit: www.shadeandshutterkeywest.com

TABLE OF CONTENTS

A LITTLE ABOUT ESSENTIAL OILS

Essential oils (EO's) are derived from shrubs, trees, flowers, roots, seeds, and leaves. They have been used since the earliest days of mankind for their soothing and healing properties. Our plant kingdom is our earliest medicine cabinet. Modern medicine uses many of the same plants.

Essential oils are derived from their sources by steam distillation, cold pressing, maceration, and pressing.

They can be used a variety of ways – diffusion into the air, inhaled (smelling, not to be confused with vaping), applied to the skin, and/or ingested. However, not every essential oil can be used in all fashions. Whether an experienced EO user or a novice, we all must take the time to educate ourselves on the potential benefits and risks of using essential oils. When it is said that an oil can only be used in a certain manner, by someone over a certain age, not around pets, etc., it is important to apply these learnings to our oil usage.

When essential oils are exposed to higher heat, they may break down some of the aromatic features of the oil, which may change its therapeutic benefit (and perhaps its flavor). You will notice that many of the recipes direct the cook to stir the oils in at the end of preparation.

It is important to use oils that are pure to ensure that nothing synthetic has been added to them. Oils that have been adulterated may have an inviting aroma, but they are not suggested for responsible use. Fortunately, there are a number of brands that are pure EO's and are readily available for purchase. Please do your research prior to purchasing essential oils.

MY COOKING WITH ESSENTIAL OILS

I started using essential oils in 2015. I was so excited about my experience with EO's, I told many family members and friends about it. It was surprising to learn how many of them had already been using EO's. None, however, were cooking with them.

One drop of lemon EO is the equivalent of the oil pressed from 8 lemon rinds, I was told. To me, that spoke of "super flavor". Loving to cook, I realized I had the flavor and healthy benefits available to me in my essential oil case. That was the brainchild for this cookbook.

Including essential oils in your food may add healthy benefits – especially when layered with fresh produce, herbs, and seasonings. Just a drop or two adds a huge boost of flavor.

Though I excel at cooking (or so I am told), I am not professionally trained as a chef and do not consider myself a true "chef". I hope I've done a good job presenting my ideas.

Folks often ask "what's your style of cooking"? My answer is "ala – in the style of." Though many of my dishes have an ethnic flair, none of these recipes are authentic to any specific group of people or geographic region. I've got a talent for combining unique flavors together, so when reading the recipes, don't be surprised if the grouping of ingredients isn't familiar to you. But once you try them, you'll be glad you did.

Please remember to season every savory recipe with salt and pepper – to your taste. It isn't always mentioned in the recipe as every person's palate is different.

I hope you enjoy these recipes. Happy Cooking!

LIST OF RECIPES WITH PAGE NUMBERS

SOUPS

SANDWICHES

MAIN ENTREES

SIDE DISHES

DESSERTS

APPETIZERS

SHRIMP COCKTAIL

½ pound medium sized cooked shrimp (shelled with the tails left on), chilled

Dipping sauce:
2 tablespoons soy sauce
2 tablespoons plus 1 teaspoon honey
Juice of a lime
¼ teaspoon cayenne (add more if you like heat)
6 drops orange essential oil
1/4 teaspoon sesame oil

Garnish:
½ tablespoon toasted sesame seeds
Cilantro, finely chopped

Lightly whisk together the soy, honey, lime juice, cayenne, orange EO, and sesame oil. Put sauce into a small bowl and place onto the middle of a platter for serving.

Assemble the shrimp around the sauce bowl. Garnish the plate with sesame seeds and cilantro

SERVES 2

continued

Shrimp Cocktail (continued)

EO BENEFIT: Orange EO may be helpful for insomnia.

HINT: It is thought that local honey can help with seasonal allergies as bees collect the pollen from local plants.

OPTIONAL SERVING IDEA: Chop the chilled shrimp, mix all ingredients and serve over mixed greens as a salad.

PORK STUFFED MUSHROOMS WITH CHEESE SAUCE

Mushrooms:
1 ten ounce package of large white button mushrooms
1 pound ground pork
¼ cup panko breadcrumbs
2 drops celery seed essential oil
½ teaspoon salt

Sauce:
1 package (5.2 ounces) Boursin® Pepper Cheese
1/3 cup half and half, milk, or cream
1 tablespoon capers, drained and smashed
3 drops lemon essential oil
2 drops black pepper essential oil

Preheat the oven to 350 degrees.

Rinse the mushrooms and pat them dry – remove all soil.
Remove the stems (save for another use).

In a bowl, gently hand mix the ground pork, bread crumbs,
celery seed EO and salt together.

Use a spoon to mound the pork into the mushroom caps. Place
the caps pork side up in a glass or metal baking dish with high
edges.

Bake for 18 minutes.

continued

Pork Stuffed Mushrooms (continued)

While the mushrooms are baking, in a small saucepan over medium low heat, add the Boursin® cheese and half of the cream. Stir occasionally, add the reminder of the cream in small amounts, stirring regularly to reach a creamy consistency. Remove sauce from heat, add the lemon and black pepper EO's.

Serve the mushrooms with the sauce spooned over the top.

SERVES 4

EO BENEFIT: Celery seed EO may help with water retention.

HINT: The cleaned mushrooms stems can be stored in a plastic bag in the refrigerator for another use, such as adding into an omelet.

OPTIONAL SERVING IDEA: Serve mushrooms and sauce over cooked pasta as an entrée.

TURKEY MEATBALLS WITH TOMATO-OLIVE SAUCE

Sauce:
¼ cup tomato paste
1 jar Italian Olive Salad (ex: Boscoli®), drained
1 ½ cups chicken stock
1 drop oregano essential oil
1 drop basil essential oil
½ teaspoon salt

Meatballs:
1 pound ground turkey
1 extra large egg, beaten until frothy
½ cup seasoned bread crumbs
3 tablespoons olive oil (or vegetable cooking oil)
Salt & Pepper

Make the sauce by adding all the sauce ingredients into a medium sized sauce pan on medium low heat, bring to a soft simmer and let cook 30 to 60 minutes. Do not let boil.

Make the meatballs - in a bowl, gently hand mix the turkey, egg, bread crumbs and salt and pepper. Roll into balls.

Heat the oil in a large skillet over medium heat. Once the oil is hot, carefully add the meatballs. Using two forks or tongs, gently turn the meatballs until browned on all sides. Add the meatballs to the sauce. Continue to simmer until meatballs are cooked through (about 8 minutes).

SERVES 4

continued

Turkey Meatballs (continued)

EO BENEFIT: Oregano EO may be helpful against arthritis.

HINT: You can reserve the olive salad brine for another use. Simply store in the jar it came in or in an airtight container in the refrigerator (up to a month).

OPTIONAL SERVING IDEA: Serve over cooked quinoa.

NACHO CUPS

1 pound ground turkey
1 small onion, peeled and minced
½ bell pepper, minced (remove seeds and ribs)
2 tablespoons olive or canola oil
¾ cup prepared salsa, drained of excess liquid
8 ounces shredded "Mexican Mix" cheese (cheese only –
        no seasonings added) (divided)
1 drop cumin essential oil
1 drop cilantro essential oil
½ - ¾ package Tostitos® Scoops™ nacho chips
2 tablespoons fresh cilantro, chopped

Preheat the oven to 400 degrees.

Heat a large skillet over medium high heat, add the oil, once
the oil is heated add the turkey, onion, and pepper. Saute,
stirring often, until the turkey is cooked through. Remove from
heat, stir in the salsa, half the cheese and EO's.

Place a single layer of chips on a rimmed baking sheet. Spoon
the turkey mixture into the Scoops™ and top with the remaining
cheese. Bake until cheese is melted (about 5 minutes).

Garnish with fresh cilantro.

EO BENEFIT: Cilantro EO may support the digestive system.

HINT: Serve with sour cream, guacamole, and
sliced green onions.

GRAPEFRUIT & FENNEL CUCUMBER CUPS

1 large English (hothouse) cucumber, cut into 1 ½" round
    pieces, (discard the ends)
1 grapefruit (preferably Ruby Red), cut supreme style and
    chopped (with juice)
2 tablespoons fennel bulb, minced
1 teaspoon Italian (flat) parsley leaves, minced
1 drop fennel essential oil
1 drop grapefruit essential oil
1 teaspoon olive or avocado oil
Salt & pepper for seasoning
2 tablespoons shelled pistachios, chopped

Using a grapefruit spoon or melon baller, carefully remove most
of the pulp from the cucumber rounds to create a "cup".

Put the cucumber pulp, grapefruit, grapefruit juice, fennel,
parsley, EO's, and oil into a bowl; stir to mix well. Season with
salt and pepper.

SERVES 2

Spoon the mixture into the cucumber cups. Garnish with
chopped nuts.

continued

Grapefruit and Fennel Cups (continued)

EO BENEFIT: Fennel EO may be helpful with urinary tract infections.

HINT: When purchasing the cucumbers, give them a slight squeeze to ensure they are firm and stand up to light pressure for ideal ripeness.

PEPPERONI SQUARES

2 tablespoons olive oil or butter
8 ounces muenster cheese, cut into small cubes
2 extra large eggs, beaten until frothy
1 cup all purpose flour
1 ½ cups milk
8 ounces pepperoni, diced
1 bell pepper (remove seeds & ribs), diced
½ teaspoon dried oregano
½ teaspoon dried basil
2 drops oregano essential oil
3 drops black pepper essential oil
2 drops basil essential oil
1/8 teaspoon salt

Heat the oven to 350. Grease the bottom of an 8 x 8 or 9 x 9 glass or ceramic casserole dish with olive oil or butter.

In a bowl, mix all ingredients (reserving 1/3 of the muenster cheese) until well blended. Pour into the greased pan and top with the reserved cheese.

Bake 45 minutes until the top is golden brown. If the top isn't browned, turn to a low broil for a few minutes watching carefully so not to burn the top.

SERVES 9 - 12

EO BENEFIT: Oregano EO may be helpful for digestive issues.

HINT: Easily doubled - bake in a 13 x 9 pan.

SALMON BRUSCHETTA

1 loaf baguette bread, cut off 12 rounds
      (reserve the remainder for another use)
2 tablespoons olive oil
1 medium garlic clove, peeled
5 ounces, smoked salmon – half diced, half flaked
2 tablespoons capers (drained)
1 hardboiled egg, minced
2 drops lemon essential oil
1 drop dill essential oil
1 teaspoon fresh dill leaves for garnish

In a bowl, gently blend together the diced salmon, cream cheese, capers, egg, and EO's. Set aside.

Preheat the oven to 375 degrees.

Brush the olive oil onto the bread rounds and place on a rimmed baking sheet.   Toast the bread rounds until crispy and lightly browned, about 8 minutes. Let cool.

Rub each round with the garlic clove to transfer the flavor onto the toast. Spread the salmon mixture atop the rounds. Garnish with flaked salmon and dill.

SERVES 4

continued

Salmon Bruschetta (continued)

EO BENEFIT: Dill EO may be helpful for asthma.

HINT: The bread can be toasted a few hours before and stored in an airtight container. The salmon mixture can be made a day ahead and stored in the refrigerator.

OPTIONAL SERVING IDEA: Garnish with grated or chopped hardboiled egg.

SALSA

1 - 1 ½ pound tomatoes, diced
½ a bell pepper, minced (about ¼ cup)
3 cloves garlic, minced (about 2 tablespoons)
1 Fresno pepper (or jalapeno pepper), seeds and ribs
        removed, minced
2 tablespoons cilantro leaves, chopped
1 tablespoon chili powder
½ teaspoon ground cumin
Dash or two of cayenne powder (adjust to your taste)
5 drops lime essential oil
4 drops lemon essential oil
Salt & pepper to taste

Mix all ingredients. Let set at least an hour before serving - mix
before serving. Can be stored in the refrigerator up to a week
in an airtight container.

EO BENEFIT: Lime essential oil may assist with weight loss.

QUESO STYLED DIP

1 bell pepper (stem, seeds, and ribs removed), finely diced
1 small onion, peeled and minced
1 large garlic clove, peeled and minced
1 stalk celery, thinly sliced
2 tablespoons butter
2 cups shredded Monterey jack cheese
1 cup shredded cheddar cheese
1 cup pepper jack cheese
2 tablespoons milk
2 cups fresh spinach (2 big handfuls), chopped
2 drops lemon essential oil
1 drop black pepper essential oil
1 drop cumin essential oil
1 ½ tablespoons butter (to grease pie plate)

Serve with nacho chips, pita chips or bread rounds.

Set oven to broil at a high temperature.

Heat a large sized skillet over medium heat; melt butter and saute pepper, onion, garlic, and celery until softened (about 5 minutes).

Change oven to bake, 425 degrees. Grease a large glass pie plate with 2 tablespoons of butter.

Add cheese, milk, spinach, and EO's to the skillet – stir well. Pour into greased pie pan. Bake until bubbly – about 20 to 25 minutes. Serve straight from the oven (with caution).

Continued

Queso Styled Dip (continued)

EO BENEFIT: Black pepper EO may be helpful for metabolism stimulation.

HINT: If the top of the dip starts to darken, turn the heat down to 375 or loosely cover the dip with foil.

OPTIONAL SERVING IDEA: Use as a sauce for cheese enchiladas. To do so, do not bake in the oven, instead keep cooking in the skillet at a very low temperature to softly simmer, stirring often, until it is creamy and hot.

SUN DRIED TOMATO HUMMUS

1 15 ounce can chickpeas (also called garbanzo beans)
¼ cup tahini, stir well before measuring
2 cloves garlic, peeled
½ a jar of sun dried tomatoes packed in oil,
      plus 2 tablespoons of the oil
Juice of half a lemon
1 drop lemon essential oil
1 drop basil essential oil
½ cup olive oil (add half first and puree, then add more a
      little at a time to reach desired consistency

Add ingredients to a food processor and puree.

Serve with assorted vegetables, pretzels, pita bread, etc.

SERVES 4

EO BENEFIT: Lemon EO may aid the circulatory system.

BEEF WONTONS

1 package wonton wrappers
2 tablespoons canola or vegetable oil
1 cup green cabbage, shredded
1 small onion, peeled and minced
1 stalk celery, diced
1 carrot, peeled and shredded
1 pound lean ground beef
1 teaspoon garlic powder
1 teaspoon salt
2 drops black pepper essential oil
3 drops celery seed essential oil
3 drops carrot seed essential oil
1 tablespoon soy sauce
Salt & pepper
½ cup water (to seal wontons)
½ - 1 cup canola or vegetable oil (to cook the wontons)

In a large skillet over medium heat, add oil. Once oil is hot add
cabbage, cook for 2 minutes. Add onion, celery, and carrot;
cook for 4 minutes. Add beef, garlic powder, and salt – cook
until beef is well crumbled and cook through. Remove from
heat and stir in EO's and soy sauce.

Let the mixture cool; season with salt and pepper. This filling
can be made ahead of time and stored in the refrigerator up to
24 hours.

Chill a rimmed baking sheet. If it doesn't fit into your
refrigerator or freezer, to chill the pan, put a plastic bag of ice
on the pan for 5 minutes (wipe off any moisture).

continued

Beef Wontons (continued)

One wonton at a time, take a wrapper and fill with a scoop of the beef mixture, fold the top over, and wet one side of the wrapper edge. The wonton wrappers are square, so you will fold them in half diagonally (after filled) to create a triangle. Press out all air and seal the wonton. Place on the chilled tray.

Line another rimmed pan (unchilled) or platter with paper towels.

In a large heavy bottom skillet, heat ½ cup of the oil until hot. Add a few wontons at a time and cook until brown and crispy on one side, then carefully turn them over and brown the other side. Using a slotted spoon, remove the cooked wontons and place on the paper towels (cover with foil to keep warm). Cook remaining wontons.

Serve the wontons hot with a dipping sauce (for example: Sweet & Sour, Thai Peanut Butter, Deli Mustard, Teriyaki)

SERVES 4 - 6

EO BENEFIT: Carrot Seed EO may be helpful against water retention.

HINT: Wonton wrappers are usually found in the produce aisle.

continued

Beef Wontons (continued)

OPTIONAL PREPARATION METHOD: Bake rather than fry.
Preheat oven to 400 degrees. Spray both sides of wontons with
cooking spray. Place wontons on a rimmed baking sheet that
has also been or sprayed with non-stick spray. Cook until golden
brown, about 7 minutes turn and cook on the opposite side until
crispy.

SMOKED TROUT DIP

1 pound smoked trout
½ cup cream cheese, softened
¼ cup plain Greek yogurt
Juice of half a lemon
2 tablespoons fresh parsley, chopped
2 tablespoons red onion, finely minced
1 drop lemon essential oil
1 drop dill essential oil
1 drop celery seed essential oil
1 drop black pepper essential oil
Salt & pepper to taste

In a bowl, flake the trout removing any pieces of skin and bone.

Add cream cheese, yogurt, and lemon juice – use a fork to cream the ingredients together. Add remaining ingredients and stir well.

Serve with nacho chips, vegetables, pita chips, crostini, etc.

SERVES 4 – 6

EO BENEFIT: Dill EO may be helpful for blood sugar regulation.

HINT: Can be made and stored in the refrigerator about a week. Stir before serving.

SHRIMP & ARTICHOKE PHYLLO CUPS

1 package frozen phyllo cups, defrosted
1/3 pound cooked shrimp, tails removed, diced
4 small artichoke hearts (from a can), drained, diced
½ small shallot, finely minced
2 ounces cream cheese, softened
1 tablespoon fresh parsley, chopped
2 drops dill essential oil
3 drops lemon essential oil
Salt to taste
Fresh dill leaves

Defrost phyllo cups by leaving package at room temperature for at least 10 minutes.

In a bowl, cream together shrimp, artichoke hearts, shallot, cream cheese, parsley, and EO's. Scoop mixture into phyllo cups.

Garnish with dill.

SERVES 4

continued

Shrimp & Artichoke Phyllo Cups (continued)

EO BENEFIT: Lemon EO may be helpful for anxiety.

HINT: Frozen, cooked shrimp can be used for this recipe.
Defrost the shrimp and use paper towels to absorb liquid.

POMEGRANATE BEEF TIPS

1 pound sirloin steak cut into 2" cubes or strips
2 tablespoons all purpose flour
½ teaspoon salt
¼ teaspoon ground pepper (or more to taste)
½ cup pomegranate juice, at room temperature
        (ex: POM® brand)
1 drop lemon essential oil
2 drops lime essential oil

2 tablespoons olive or vegetable oil

2 tablespoons fresh parsley, chopped
Salt & Pepper

In a plastic bag, add the flour, salt and pepper - shake to blend. Add the beef tips and shake to coat with the flour.

Heat a large skillet on medium high heat, add the oil. Once the oil is hot, shake the beef free of flour and add the beef to the pan (save the flour). Sear the beef tips for 2 minutes on all sides (about 8 minutes total). Using a slotted spoon, move the beef from the pan to a plate. Cover the beef with foil to keep warm.

Add the remaining flour in the bag into the pan; stir until it starts to thicken, scraping the bottom of the pan. If needed, add another tablespoon of olive or vegetable oil. Add the pomegranate juice and EO's. Cook and stir for another minute until heated through.

continued

Pomegranate Beef Tips (continued)

Remove the pan from the heat and add the beef tips back into the pan. Stir quickly to coat the beef tips. Plate the beef tips and garnish with chopped parsley and season with salt and pepper.

SERVES 4 - 6

EO BENEFIT: Lime essential oil may be helpful for weight loss.

HINT: Choose a quality piece of steak for best flavor and tenderness.

OPTIONAL SERVING IDEA: Serve in a radicchio cup (as shown).

ASIAN STYLED CHICKEN DUMPLINGS

1 package wonton wrappers
2 tablespoons canola or vegetable oil
1 cup green cabbage, shredded
1 shallot, peeled and minced
5 water chestnuts (from a can), drained and minced
1 carrot, peeled and shredded
1 pound ground chicken
½ teaspoon garlic powder
½ teaspoon salt
1 drop black pepper essential oil
1 drop orange essential oil
1 drop carrot seed essential oil

½ cup water (to seal wontons)

Soy sauce

In a large skillet over medium heat, add oil. Once oil is hot add cabbage, cook for 2 minutes. Add shallot and carrot; cook for 4 minutes. Add chicken, garlic powder, and salt – cook until chicken is well crumbled and cooked through, about 8 – 10 minutes. Stir in water chestnuts. Remove from heat and stir in EO's. Let the mixture cool (can be made and stored in the refrigerator a day ahead).

Chill a rimmed baking sheet. If it doesn't fit into your refrigerator or freezer to chill it, put a plastic bag of ice on the pan for 5 minutes (wipe off any moisture).

continued

The wonton wrappers are square, so you will fold them in half diagonally (after filling) to create a triangle. One wonton at a time, take a wrapper and fill with a scoop of the chicken mixture, fold the top over, and wet one side of the wrapper edge. Press out all air and seal the dumpling. Place on the chilled tray.

In a large heavy skillet or Dutch oven, bring 4 inches of water to a boil, then reduce to simmer. Once water is simmering, add a few wontons at a time and cook until the wrapper is softened (about 3 minutes). Using a slotted spoon, remove the cooked wontons and place in a bowl (cover with foil to keep warm). Cook remaining dumplings. Serve hot drizzled with soy sauce.

SERVES 4 - 6

EO BENEFIT: Orange EO may be helpful against insomnia.

HINT: Onion or leek can be used in place of the shallot.

OPTIONAL SERVING IDEA: Serve the dumplings with a dipping sauce, for example: Sweet & Sour, Thai Peanut Butter, Deli Mustard, Teriyaki

LEMON PEPPER CHICKEN WINGS

1 pound chicken wings & drummettes
1 teaspoon salt
½ teaspoon freshly cracked black pepper
2 tablespoons vegetable or olive oil
10 drops lemon essential oil
5 drops black pepper essential oil

Preheat oven to 400 degrees.

In a bowl or plastic zip bag, toss the wings with salt and pepper.
Mix the oils and pour over the chicken wings – toss to coat.
Place the wings in a single layer on a rimmed baking sheet.
Bake for 20 - 25 minutes until completely cooked. Turn the
oven onto broil and cook to desired crispness.

SERVES 2-3

EO BENEFIT: Black pepper EO may be helpful for fatigue.

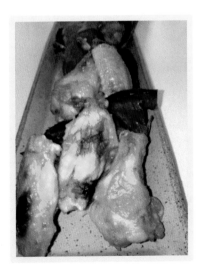

BEEF TARTARE

¾ pound USDA choice or prime grade beef tenderloin,
    minced or diced
2 tablespoons good quality extra virgin olive oil
1 drop lemon essential oil
1 drop rosemary essential oil
1 teaspoon ground mustard
1 small shallot, peeled and minced
1 tablespoon capers, drained and chopped
1 tablespoon chives, chopped

SERVES 4

Gently mix all ingredients in a glass or ceramic bowl (can be prepared up to 4 hours ahead of time – keep refrigerated until ready to eat).

Serve with either toast points, baguette bread, bread crisps, pita chips, rye bread rounds or water crackers.

EO BENEFIT: Rosemary EO may help with memory issues.

HINT: The meat will slice and chop easier if put into the freezer for 20 minutes prior to handling it.

OPTIONAL SERVING IDEA: Add 3 chopped anchovy fillets – rinse and pat them dry before chopping.

SALADS

CITRUS CHICKEN SALAD

1 pound boneless, skinless chicken breast
Juice of one lemon and 2" of rind
Juice of one orange and 2" of rind
1 large garlic clove, peeled and sliced in half
4 sprigs fresh tarragon
2 oranges, cut supreme style
½ cup frozen peas, defrosted
3 tablespoons red onion, peeled and minced
1 cup plain Greek yogurt
1 drop juniper essential oil
1 drop orange essential oil
1 drop grapefruit essential oil
1 drop lemon essential oil
2 tablespoons apple cider vinegar
1 tablespoon honey
Dash cayenne
Shake of garlic powder
Shake of onion powder

SERVES 4

Put the chicken, lemon juice, orange juice, rinds, and 2 sprigs
of tarragon in a 3 quart sauce pan. Cover with water. Bring to
a boil, cover, reduce heat to low and simmer for 12 – 15 minutes
until the chicken is cooked through. Remove the chicken from
the liquid and chill for 2 hours or overnight. Once chilled, chop
the chicken into bite sized pieces.

continued

Citrus Chicken Salad (continued)

In a bowl, add the cooked and chilled chicken, the orange segments, peas, and red onion.

In a separate bowl, whisk together the yogurt, EO's, vinegar, seasonings, and reserved orange juice. Pour over the chicken mixture and fold to coat. Garnish with leaves of 2 sprigs of tarragon, chopped.

EO BENEFIT: Juniper EO may be helpful for urinary tract and bladder infections.

OPTIONAL SERVING IDEA: Serve as a wrap sandwich.

CAPRESE SALAD

2 pints cherry, grape, or small heirloom tomatoes –
      sliced into small wedges
2 tablespoons minced basil leaves
16 ounces fresh mozzarella, cut into small wedges
¼ cup extra virgin olive oil
2 – 3 tablespoons white balsamic vinegar
1 drop basil essential oil
2 drops lemon essential oil
4 drops black pepper essential oil
Finishing salt (ex: sea salt)

Put tomatoes and mozzarella into a medium sized bowl.

In a separate bowl or measuring cup, whisk together olive oil, balsamic vinegar, and essential oils.

Pour the dressing over the tomato mixture and gently fold to coat. Use a slotted spoon to plate – reserve extra dressing for another use, or spoon additional dressing over the salad.

Sprinkle with finishing salt.

SERVES 2 - 4

EO BENEFIT: Basil EO may be helpful for migraines.

HINT: Fresh mozzarella can be purchased already cut into rounds.

MEDITERRANEAN QUINOA SALAD

2 ½ cups cooked quinoa
2 cups assorted roasted vegetables
     (ex: peppers, onions, eggplant, tomato) (can be
     purchased in a jar and drained)
½ cup crumbled feta cheese
½ cup extra virgin olive oil
¼ cup red wine vinegar
1 tablespoon capers, drained
1 drop oregano essential oil
2 drops grapefruit essential oil
2 drops lemon essential oil
1 tablespoon celery greens, chopped (optional)
¼ cup toasted pine nuts or roasted pistachio nuts, chopped

Place quinoa and vegetables in a serving bowl.

In a separate bowl, whisk together feta, olive oil, vinegar, capers, and EOs. Use the back of a spoon to mash the feta and capers. Pour over the quinoa mixture and fold in.

Garnish with celery greens and nuts.

SERVES 4

continued

Mediterranean Quinoa Salad (continued)

EO BENEFIT: Grapefruit EO oil may help for liver disorders.

HINT: Cook quinoa in vegetable stock rather than plain water for additional flavor.

OPTIONAL SERVING IDEA: Add 8 ounces cooked chicken or shrimp.

CHOPPED TUNA SALAD

12 ounce can of chunk light tuna packed in water, drained
½ cup romaine leaves, chopped
2 tablespoon red onion, peeled and minced
2 tablespoons bell pepper, ribs and seeds discarded, diced
1 stalk celery, diced
1 medium tomato, seeded and chopped
1/3 cup mayonnaise (or more to your preference)
1 drop dill essential oil
2 drops celery seed essential oil
Onion powder, dash
Garlic powder, dash
1 tablespoon fresh dill, chopped
Salt & Pepper

SERVES 3-4

Mix all ingredients together. Suggested: add mayonnaise a bit at a time to reach the consistency you desire.

EO BENEFIT: Celery seed EO may be helpful for digestive issues.

HINT: You can also use tuna packed in oil; be sure to drain it well.

OPTIONAL SERVING IDEA: Spoon into romaine lettuce leaf "cups" and serve as rolls.

EGG SALAD

6 hard boiled eggs, shelled and chopped
1 large stalk celery with greens, minced
2 tablespoons red onion, peeled and minced
¼ cup plain Greek yogurt (or mayonnaise)
1 teaspoon fresh dill, chopped
1 drop dill essential oil
1 drop celery seed essential oil
1 drop black pepper essential oil
Salt & Pepper

SERVES 3-4

In a bowl, mix all ingredients. Refrigerate at least an hour. Can be stored up to a week in the refrigerator.

Serve atop a prepared garden salad, with crackers, on bread, or however you may like it.

EO BENEFIT: Dill EO may help ease menstrual cramps.

HINT: Cooked and shelled hard boiled eggs can be purchased in the dairy aisle.

OPTIONAL SERVING IDEA: Core 4 medium to large tomatoes and spoon the salad into the tomatoes.

ROASTED BEET SALAD WITH
WALNUT VINAIGRETTE

1 ½ pounds beets, scrubbed and greens removed
      (reserve greens for another use)
¼ cup balsamic vinegar
½ cup walnut oil
2 drops lemon essential oil
2 drops tangerine essential oil
4 ounces goat cheese crumbled (halved)
½ a medium shallot, peeled
2 tablespoons shelled walnuts, chopped
Bibb lettuce (aka Boston Bibb), rinsed and patted dry,
      separated into "cups"

SERVES 4

Roast the beets: Preheat the oven to 400 degrees. Wrap each beet in aluminum foil and place on a rimmed baking sheet. Depending on the size of the beets, roast from 50 to 70 minutes until softened (a knife should easily slide into the beet center). Remove from the oven and let cool until able to safely handle the beets. Remove the beets from the foil. Use a paring knife to skin the beets, and chop into 1 ½" pieces. The beets can be roasted and put aside in the refrigerator up to a day prior to using (let come up to room temperature before serving).

In a blender or small food processor make the dressing: vinegar, EOs, half the goat cheese, the shallot, and salt & pepper.

continued

Place a lettuce leaf on each serving plate (or in a circle on a platter), spoon the beets atop and drizzle dressing over the vegetables. Garnish with remaining cheese and walnuts.

EO BENEFIT: Tangerine EO may be helpful for irritability.

HINT: To avoid staining your cutting board while chopping the cooked beets, put down a barrier first (ex: parchment paper, foil, wax paper, etc.)

BALSAMIC GREEN BEAN SALAD

1 pound fresh green beans, rinsed and ends removed
1 large garlic clove, peeled and minced
1 medium red onion, peeled and cut into thin slices
2 tablespoons olive oil
2 tablespoons cold water
1 tablespoon walnut oil
2 drops lemon essential oil
2 tablespoons balsamic vinegar

SERVES 4

Heat a large skillet over medium heat. Once hot, add olive oil.
Once the oil is hot, add the beans, garlic and onion - cook for
about 8 minutes until garlic and onion are softened and beans
begin to cook.

Add water to pan to steam the beans. Once beans are cooked
to desire tenderness, remove from heat and stir in walnut oil,
EO, and vinegar. Toss to coat. Can be served warm or cold.

EO BENEFIT: Lemon EO may be helpful for circulatory problems.

HINT: To cook the beans al dente (firm to the bite) so they
have a bit of a crunch, cook for just a 2-3 minutes.

OPTIONAL SERVING IDEA: Garnish with crispy bacon bits.

SALMON - AVOCADO SALAD

2 ounces cooked, cooled salmon filet
½ avocado, diced
1 teaspoon minced red onion (optional)
1 teaspoon mayonnaise
1 drop lemon essential oil
1 drop cilantro oil
Salt & pepper
Garnish with chopped fresh parsley (if desired)

SERVES 1

Flake the salmon into a bowl. Add the remaining ingredients and fold until smooth.

EO BENEFIT: Lemon EO may be helpful for anxiety.

HINT: If making more than one serving, add additional essential oil sparingly, tasting before adding more EOs to ensure their flavors don't overpower the dish.

ASIAN STYLE SALAD WITH PORK

Marinade and dressing:
3 tablespoons rice wine vinegar
1/2 cup vegetable oil
Juice of a lemon
1 drop lemon essential oil
2 drops lime essential oil
2 drops cilantro essential oil
1 drop black pepper essential oil
1/8 teaspoon sesame oil
2 teaspoons soy sauce

1 tablespoon tahini paste

1 head napa cabbage, sliced into shreds
4 scallions, sliced (both white and green parts)
1 large carrot, peeled and shredded
¼ cup red onion, peeled and chopped (or more to taste)
1 red bell pepper, ribs and seeds removed, diced
2 stalks celery, thinly sliced
2 tablespoons cilantro, chopped
1 small jalapeno, ribs and seeds removed, minced

Optional:
¼ cup chopped nuts (peanuts, almonds, or cashews)
1 tablespoon toasted sesame seeds

1 pound boneless pork loin chops, fat removed

SERVES 4

continued

Asian Style Salad with Pork (continued)

Preheat oven to 350 degrees.

In a glass or ceramic measuring cup, mix all marinade/dressing ingredients EXCEPT tahini paste. Pour half of the mixture into a plastic bag. Add the pork and marinate for 30 minutes to 1 hour. Set aside remaining marinade/dressing.

Bake the pork chops for 25 minutes. Once cooked, remove from heat, and let rest 4 minutes. Thinly slice the meat.

While the pork is cooking, prepare all vegetables and place in a large bowl.

Add the tahini paste to the remaining marinade/dressing and mix well. Pour over vegetables and toss well. Plate with cooked pork atop the salad garnished with nuts and sesame seeds.

EO BENEFIT: Cilantro EO may be helpful for detoxification.

HINT: Pork should be cooked to no less than medium well in temperature. Cook longer than 25 minutes if necessary.

OPTIONAL SERVING IDEA: If preferred, chicken, duck, or shrimp can be substituted for pork.

MELON & CRISPY PANCETTA SALAD WITH
BLEU CHEESE VINAIGRETTE

1/4 pound pancetta, cut into cubes
4 large leaves basil, cut into thin strips
2 tablespoons white balsamic vinegar
½ cup bleu cheese crumbles
¾ cup olive oil
2 drops lemon essential oil
1 drop black pepper essential oil
3 drops basil essential oil
4 cups greens (ex: spring mix, frisee, arugla, endive,
        chicory), cleaned and chopped
One honey dew or cantaloupe melon, peeled, seeded & cut
        into chunks

SERVES 4

In a hot skillet over medium heat, cook the pancetta until
crispy. Reserve 1 tablespoon of the rendered fat.

In a blender or food processor, puree vinegar, bleu cheese,
reserved rendered pancetta fat, olive oil, and EOs until smooth.

Toss greens with 1/3 dressing (dress with caution - gently coat
the greens).

Place on 4 serving plates. Toss melon in 1/3 of the dressing
(add dressing slowly so that it is coated to your desire) and
place atop the greens.

continued

Melon & Crispy Pancetta Salad (continued)

Sprinkle basil and pancetta over the salad, serve with the remaining dressing on the side.

EO BENEFIT: Basil EO may be helpful for throat infections.

HINT: When ordering the pancetta at the deli department, ask that it be cut into two thick pieces.

FRUIT SALAD WITH YOGURT DRESSING

2 apples, cored and diced into 1" pieces
1 ½ cups red grapes, sliced in half
½ pint blueberries or blackberries
2 kiwi, peeled and sliced into half rounds
¼ cup chopped walnuts

Dressing:
1 cup plain Greek yogurt
2 tablespoons honey
Juice of half a lemon
2 tablespoons apple cider vinegar
1 drop cinnamon essential oil
1 drop basil essential oil

One tablespoon fresh basil, minced for garnish (optional)

SERVES 4

Add all the fruit to a bowl.

In a blender, shaker or small food processor, add all dressing ingredients and mix until smooth. Pour dressing over the fruit just prior to serving and stir gently in so that all fruit is evenly coated. Gently mix in walnuts. Garnish with basil.

EO BENEFIT: Cinnamon EO may be helpful for ulcers.

HINT: Peel the apple if desired.

OPTIONAL SERVING IDEA: Replace the walnuts with pecans.

KALE-APPLE SALAD

Juice of ½ a lemon
1 tablespoon apple cider vinegar
1 drop lemon essential oil
1 drop fennel essential oil
2 tablespoons olive oil
2 ½ ounces baby kale
½ a large Granny Smith apple, cored and cut
      into matchsticks
¼ cup dried prunes or figs, diced
¼ cup slivered almonds, toasted
2 tablespoons freshly grated Asiago or Parmesan cheese

SERVES 2

Whisk lemon juice, apple cider vinegar, essential oils and olive oil together in a bowl. Add the kale and toss well.

Add apple, prunes or figs, and almonds; toss to evenly coat all ingredients. Garnish with grated cheese.

EO BENEFIT: Fennel EO may be helpful for diabetes.

TEX MEX SHREDDED CHICKEN SALAD

1 rotisserie chicken, meat removed and shredded
1 head romaine lettuce, cleaned and chopped
1 14 ounce can corn niblets, drained
1 green bell pepper, diced (discard seeds, ribs, and stem)
¼ cup red onion, chopped
4 scallions, sliced (white and green parts)
1 can black beans, drained and rinsed
¾ cup prepared salsa
¾ cup sour cream or plain Greek yogurt
1 drop cumin essential oil
1 drop cilantro essential oil
2 drops lime essential oil
Salt & Pepper

SERVES 4

Place all ingredients in a large bowl and gently toss well to coat.
Season with salt and pepper.

EO BENEFIT: Cumin EO may be helpful to reduce bloating.

HINT: Fresh or frozen can may be substituted for canned corn.

OPTIONAL SERVING IDEA: Spoon and roll mixture into flavored
tortillas for a sandwich.

SHRIMP AND ORANGE SALAD

1 pound cooked shrimp (medium sized), all shells removed
2 medium sweet oranges, peeled and cut supreme style
      (cut over a bowl to reserve the juice)
3 green onions (scallions), thinly sliced
      (white and green parts)
½ red bell pepper, seeded and diced
2 tablespoons shallot or red onion, minced
3 tablespoons walnut or avocado oil
¼ cup plain Greek yogurt
1 drop orange essential oil
1 drop cilantro essential oil
1 drop lemon essential oil
1 drop black pepper essential oil
Salt & Pepper to taste
4 cups fresh spinach leaves

SERVES 4

Place shrimp, oranges, scallions, pepper and shallot in a bowl. Mix orange juice, essential oils and yogurt together.

Combine the shrimp and orange mixture by gently tossing to coat well.

Refrigerate 30 minutes to 2 hours before serving.

Spoon shrimp mixture over spinach leaves.

continued

Shrimp and Orange Salad (continued)

EO BENEFIT: Orange EO may be helpful for hypertension.

HINT: Cooked shrimp can be purchased frozen. Defrost before using.

OPTIONAL SERVING IDEA: Replace cooked shrimp with breaded shrimp. Serve the breaded shrimp hot atop the salad.

WARM ITALIAN BEEF SALAD

8 cups salad greens (ex: Romaine, ice berg, Spring Mix)
1 pound top round steak, sliced across the grain into
        1" thick pieces (fat removed)
1 medium red or green pepper, seeded and de-ribbed and
        cut into thin strips
1 small yellow or white onion, peeled and cut into
        thin strips
2 tablespoons extra virgin olive or vegetable oil
1/3 cup extra virgin olive oil
3 tablespoons red wine vinegar
1 drop lemon essential oil
2 drops oregano essential oil
1 drop basil essential oil

Garnish:
¼ cup banana peppers, drained
¼ cup pitted Kalamata olives, sliced in half
¼ cup grated parmesan cheese

Optional (add as many as you'd like):
1 tomato, chopped
4 radishes, sliced
½ cucumber, sliced

SERVES 4

Divide your salad greens among 4 large plates or salad bowls.
Set aside.

continued

Warm Italian Beef Salad (continued)

Salt & pepper the sliced beef. Heat a medium sized skillet over medium heat; add the oil. Once the oil is hot, saute the peppers and onions for 3 minutes, turn the temperature up to medium high, add the beef and cook for another 5 minutes. Remove the pan from the heat, and stir in extra virgin olive oil, vinegar, roasted garlic, and EO's. Toss well.

Serve cooked beef atop the salad greens garnish as desired.

EO BENEFIT: Basil EO may be helpful for menstrual cramping.

HINT: Put the beef in the freezer for 20 minutes, it will make slicing it easier.

OPTIONAL SERVING IDEA: Omit the salad greens and spoon the beef mixture into hoagie rolls, top with a slice of provolone cheese and put under the broiler until the cheese is melted.

MOROCCAN STYLED CHICKEN SALAD

1 pound cooked chicken breast, chopped into 1" pieces
1/3 cup pitted Kalamata olives, diced
¼ cup dried dates or figs, minced
¼ cup golden raisins
¼ sliced or slivered almonds, toasted
¾ cup plain Greek yogurt
1 teaspoon mild curry powder
3 drops lemon essential oil
2 drops cilantro essential oil

SERVES 4

Place chicken, olives, raisins, and almonds into a bowl.

Mix yogurt, curry powder and EO's until well blended. Pour yogurt dressing over chicken mixture, and gently stir.

Refrigerate 30 minutes to 2 hours before serving.

If the mixture seems dry, stir in either a tablespoon of olive oil or cold water.

EO BENEFIT: Lemon EO may be helpful for obesity.

SOUPS

COLD CREAMY MANGO SOUP

1 jalapeno
1/4 cup plain Greek yogurt or regular plain yogurt
2 mangoes - peeled, pitted, and cut into cubes OR a
       16 ounce bag frozen mango - defrosted
2 cups orange juice
1 ½ cups plain Greek yogurt or regular plain yogurt
4 drops lime essential oil
2 drops tangerine essential oil
4 drops grapefruit essential oil
4 large basil leaves chopped - for garnish

SERVES 4

Over medium high heat in a dry skillet, cook the jalapeno until it is charred on all sides and softened. Once cool enough to handle, remove seeds and ribs, and mince. Mix half the jalapeno with ¼ cup yogurt and set aside.

In a food processor or with a wand blender, puree the mango, orange juice, other half of the jalapeno, with 1 ½ cups yogurt. Blend until very smooth. Chill for 3 hours. Prior to serving, add the essential oils and mix well.

Serve garnished with basil leaves and a dollop of reserved jalapeno yogurt.

Optional garnish: drizzle a small bit of avocado oil atop the soup.

continued

Cold Creamy Mango Soup (continued)

EO BENEFIT: Grapefruit essential oil may be helpful for liver disorders.

HINT: Mango puree can be made up to a day ahead and stored in the refrigerator. Re-mix with the blender and add more yogurt if needed for a smooth consistency.

OPTIONAL SERVING IDEA: Put mixture into an ice cream maker for a delicious dessert.

TOMATO SOUP WITH GRILLED CHEESE CROUTONS

Soup:
1 medium onion, chopped
2 medium cloves garlic, chopped
1 28 ounce can whole or crushed tomatoes
1 ½ cups V-8® juice or tomato juice
1 tablespoon agave nectar or 1 tablespoon sugar
1 teaspoon salt (or more to taste)
1 drop basil essential oil
1 drop oregano essential oil
1 drop lemongrass essential oil
1 drop celery seed essential oil
1 drop black pepper essential oil

Croutons:
4 slices of bread (any sliced bread will do, but
        Rye bread is recommended)
4 tablespoons butter
2 thick slices of cheese (ex: Havarti, Gouda, Cheddar)
4 tablespoons butter

In a large sauce pan over medium heat, melt the better – add the onion and garlic. Cook until softened, about 5 minutes. Add all the remaining ingredients except the EOs. Bring to a soft boil, then reduce heat and simmer about 40 minutes.

Before serving the soup, add the EOs and stir well. Use an emersion blender to puree the soup (or carefully blend the hot mixture in a blender in batches if necessary).

continued

Make a grilled cheese sandwich: heat a skillet to medium heat, butter one slice of bread and place it butter side down in the skillet. Place the cheese on top. Butter the other slice of bread and place it butter side up on top of the cheese. Cook until browned, flip and cook the other side until browned. Remove to a plate. Cut into small "croutons".

Serve in a bowl topped with grilled cheese croutons.

SERVES 4

EO BENEFIT: Lemongrass EO may be helpful for bladder infections.

HINT: Use rye bread and Havarti cheese for unique croutons.

TURKEY TACO SOUP

2 tablespoons olive oil
1 ½ pounds ground turkey (85% fat)
1 small onion, minced
1 bell pepper (any color), cored, seeded and diced
1 large clove garlic, peeled and minced
2 jalapeno or serrano peppers, cored, seeded and minced
48 ounces chicken stock
4 ½ ounce can of green chiles – with liquid
11 ounce can of corn niblets – drained
14 ½ ounce can diced tomatoes – with liquid
2 tablespoons diced pimiento (optional)
2 drops lime essential oil
2 drops cumin essential oil
2 drops cilantro essential oil
Salt & Pepper (to taste)
Cilantro leaves, chopped for garnish
Sour cream for garnish
Crushed nacho chips for garnish

SERVES 4

In a large pot over medium high heat, add the oil and ground turkey. Cook and stir until the turkey starts to brown (3 – 4 minutes). Add the onion, bell pepper, garlic, and jalapeno/serrano peppers. Reduce the heat to medium, cook stirring the ingredients until the onions soften (3 minutes).

continued

Turkey Taco Soup (continued)

Add stock, chiles, corn, and tomatoes – turn the heat up to medium high until the mixture comes to a soft boil, then turn it down to a simmer. Add essential oils and let simmer 30 minutes to 1 hour.

Season with salt and pepper to taste (the nacho chips will be salty, so use caution when adding salt.)

Garnish the soup with chopped cilantro, crushed nacho chips, and a dollop of sour cream.

EO BENEFIT: Lime essential oil may help to boost the immune system.

HINT: Plain Greek yogurt can be used in place of sour cream.

OPTIONAL SERVING IDEA: Puree the mixture and use as a sauce for enchiladas.

CARIBBEAN SHRIMP SOUP

2 tablespoons olive oil
1 yam or sweet potato, peeled and diced into ½" pieces
1 small onion, peeled, halved and thinly sliced
1 stalk celery with greens, diced
2 cloves garlic, peeled and minced
2 strands saffron
1 drop lime essential oil
2 drops nutmeg essential oil
1 drop clove essential oil
32 ounces coconut milk
1 jar clam juice or 1 teaspoon Better Than Bouillon®
      fish or lobster paste
1 pound small cooked shrimp (shells and tails removed)
½ cup unsweetened shredded coconut, toasted

SERVES 4

Heat a large sauce pan over medium heat, once hot, add the olive oil. Saute yam, onion, celery, and garlic until softened (about 5 minutes) (reduce heat if garlic starts to brown). Season with salt and pepper.

Add remaining ingredients (except shrimp) and stir well. Increase heat to medium high and bring to a soft boil. Reduce heat to low and let simmer for at least a half hour and up to an hour.

Prior to serving, mix in shrimp to warm through.

Serve with garnish of toasted coconut.

continued

Caribbean Shrimp Soup (continued)

EO BENEFIT: Nutmeg EO may be helpful for ulcers.

HINT: If using raw shrimp, peel, devein and remove tails. Stir into hot soup until cooked through.

OPTIONAL SERVING IDEA: Before adding the shrimp, use an emulsion blender to puree the soup so it is chowder-like.

YUCATAN STYLED PORK STEW

2 tablespoons vegetable or olive oil
1 ½ pounds pork loin, fat trimmed and cut into 1" cubes
Salt & Pepper
1 large dry ancho chili
2 cups water
1 large yellow or white onion, peeled, halved and cut
       into thin slivers
3 cloves garlic, peeled and minced
3 large carrots, cut into 2" thick rounds (peels can be
       removed if desired)
1 bay leaf
1 medium jalapeno pepper, seeded and chopped
Juice of one lime
2 drops clove essential oil
2 drops lime essential oil
1 drop cilantro essential oil
3 roma or plum tomatoes, cut into quarters
32 ounces chicken stock
2 tablespoons chopped cilantro for garnish (optional)

SERVES 4

Season the pork with salt and pepper and set aside.

Bring 2 cups water to a boil. Submerge the dry ancho chili for 5
minutes. Let cool, remove the stem and put into a blender or
food processor. Keep the water aside.
In the blender or food processor, blend until smooth the ancho
chili, jalapeno, lime juice, EOs and half the tomatoes.

continued

If you need more liquid, add some of some of the chili water until smooth and creamy. Set aside.

Heat a heavy stock pan or Dutch oven on medium high heat. Once the pan is hot, add the oil. Once the oil is hot, add the seasoned pork and cook until browned on all sides.

Using a slotted pan, remove the pork from the pan and set aside.

Reduce heat to medium low. Add the onions, garlic, carrots and bay leaf (add another tablespoon of oil if needed to keep vegetables moving). Cook stirring regularly about 5 minutes until vegetables start to soften.

Pour the blended mixture and the chicken stock into the pan with the vegetables. Add the pork with any juices that accumulated. Bring to a soft boil and reduce heat to low. Simmer at least an hour and up to two hours stirring often.

Prior to serving, season with salt and pepper. Garnish with cilantro.

EO BENEFIT: Clove EO may be helpful for diabetes.

HINT: When cooking the pork, do not crowd the pan. Cook in batches if necessary.

OPTIONAL SERVING IDEA: Spoon soup over cooked rice.

GREEN GAZPACHO

2 seedless (aka hothouse) cucumbers, cubed
1 jalapeno pepper, roasted (discard seeds, ribs, and stem),
    sliced
1 green bell pepper, roasted (discard seeds, ribs, and
    stem), sliced
3 tomatillos, skins removed
2 cloves garlic, peeled and sliced
1 Hass avocado (discard skin and pit), cubed
¼ cup fresh parsley leaves
3 drops lime essential oil
2 drops cumin essential oil
2 drops celery seed essential oil
1 drop cilantro essential oil
1 cup purified or filtered water
1 teaspoon salt

SERVES 4

In a food processor or blender, process all ingredients until
smooth. Serve chilled

EO BENEFIT: Celery seed EO may be helpful for arthritis.

BEEF VEGETABLE SOUP

2 tablespoons vegetable or olive oil
1 ½ pounds beef stew meat, excess fat trimmed and cut
      into 1" cubes
Salt & Pepper
1 large yellow or white onion, peeled, halved and cut into
      thin slivers
3 cloves garlic, peeled and minced
3 carrots, peeled and cut into 2" thick rounds
2 large celery stalks with greens, sliced thinly
2 russet potatoes, cut into 2" pieces (peel if desired)
Corn niblets from 2 ears of corn (1 cup)
1 cup frozen sweet peas
1 bay leaf
3 tablespoons tomato paste
32 ounces beef stock
32 ounces vegetable stock
2 drops thyme essential oil
2 drops oregano essential oil
2 drops black pepper essential oil
1 drop lemon essential oil
2 tablespoons chopped parsley for garnish (optional)

SERVES 4 - 6

Season the beef with salt and pepper and set aside.

continued

Beef Vegetable Soup (continued)

Heat a heavy stock pan or Dutch oven on medium high heat. Once the pan is hot, add the oil. Once the oil is hot, add the seasoned beef (do not crowd the pan - cook in batches if necessary) and cook until browned on all sides. Using a slotted pan, remove the beef from the pan and set aside.

Reduce heat to medium low. Add the onions, garlic, carrots, celery, and bay leaf (add another tablespoon of oil if needed to keep vegetables moving). Cook stirring regularly about 5 minutes until vegetables start to soften.

Add the corn, peas, and tomato paste into the pan and mix well for 1 minute. Add stock, EOs, and seared beef (include any juices that accumulated from the beef). Bring to a soft boil and reduce heat to low. Simmer at least an hour and up to two hours stirring often.

Prior to serving, season with salt and pepper. Garnish with chopped parsley.

EO BENEFIT: Thyme EO may be helpful for hepatitis.

HINT: Fresh corn can be replaced with 1 cup frozen corn or a 15.25 ounce can corn niblets (drained).

OPTIONAL SERVING IDEA: Add ½ cup uncooked quinoa to the pan after adding the stock.

CHICKEN LEMON PESTO SOUP

2 tablespoons olive oil
1 medium sweet onion, peeled and diced
2 cloves garlic, peeled and minced
32 ounces chicken stock
5 fresh basil leaves
2 tablespoons pine nuts
Juice of a lemon
1 tablespoon olive oil
4 drops lemon essential oil
2 drops basil essential oil
2 cups shredded cooked chicken
2 cups fresh spinach leaves
2 large pieces of roasted red pepper
     (ex: from a jar), drained and chopped
Grated Parmesan cheese for garnish

SERVES 4

Heat a Dutch oven or large soup pan on medium heat, once hot add 2 tablespoons olive oil. Once the oil is heated reduce the heat to medium low, add onion and garlic - saute and sweat for 5 minutes.

In a blender or food processor, puree basil, pine nuts, lemon juice and essential oils. Add to the pot along with all remaining ingredients except the grated parmesan cheese.

Bring to a boil, the reduce heat to low and let simmer for half an hour.

continued

Chicken Lemon Pesto Soup (continued)

Before serving, season with salt and pepper. Serve garnished with parmesan cheese.

EO BENEFIT: Basil EO may be helpful for lung infections.

HINT: Use the breasts from a prepared rotisserie chicken.

PORK & CABBAGE SOUP

1 pound ground pork
1 pound pork tenderloin, excess fat removed,
        cut into 1 ½" pieces
2 tablespoons olive or vegetable oil
1 tablespoon paprika
1 medium white or yellow onion, peeled and diced
4 cloves garlic, peeled and minced
3 leeks, sliced (white and light green tender parts)
1 small head green cabbage, shredded
2 cups sauerkraut, drain away half the liquid
1 tablespoon caraway seeds
2 drops dill essential oil
2 drops black pepper essential oil
2 drops coriander essential oil
32 ounces chicken stock
14 ounces vegetable stock
1 teaspoon salt

SERVES 4

Heat a large soup pan or Dutch oven atop the stove at medium heat. Once the pan is hot, add the ground pork and cook through. Remove cooked meat and fat from the pan and set aside.

Heat the oil in the pan and add the tenderloin cubes and paprika, sear on all sides (about 5 minutes). Reduce the heat to medium low and add the onion, garlic, leeks, and cabbage. Cook until the vegetables are softened (about 10 minutes) stirring often.

continued

Pork & Cabbage Soup (continued)

Strain the cooked ground beef to remove the extra fat, and add the meat to the pan along with all the remaining ingredients. Increase heat to medium high and bring to a boil. Reduce heat to low and simmer for at least one hour and up to two hours.

EO BENEFIT: Coriander EO may be helpful for intestinal issues.

HINT: Shredded cabbage can be purchased already shredded in the produce aisle.

OPTIONAL SERVING IDEA: Instead of green cabbage, replace with a bag of prepared cole slaw mix.

DIJON SHRIMP SOUP

1 pound medium sized shrimp, tails removed & deveined,
    chopped into ½" pieces
2 tablespoons olive oil
1 medium sweet onion, peeled and minced
1 clove garlic, peeled and minced
½ bell pepper (stem, seeds & ribs removed), diced
1 leek, thinly sliced (discard course tough tops of the leek)
Salt & Pepper
¼ cup Dijon mustard
32 ounces vegetable stock
4 cups fresh spinach (4 heaping handfuls)
2 drops basil essential oil
3 drops rosemary essential oil

SERVES 4

In a large soup pan, heat olive oil on medium heat. Once the oil is hot, reduce the heat to medium low, and add onions, garlic, pepper and leek - season with salt & pepper.

Cook until vegetables have softened (about 5 minutes). Add mustard and vegetable stock to the pan; stir well.

Bring to a light boil on medium high heat, reduce heat and let simmer for a half hour.

Add shrimp and spinach. Stir until shrimp is cooked through - about 3 minutes. Remove from heat and add EO's.

continued

Dijon Shrimp Soup (continued)

EO BENEFIT: Rosemary EO may be helpful for impaired memory.

HINT: Use a small bag of frozen cooked shrimp in place of raw shrimp. Stir into the soup 5 minutes before serving to heat through.

OPTIONAL SERVING IDEA: Serve spooned over cooked rice.

MEATBALL SOUP

1 ½ pounds ground beef
½ cup panko bread crumbs
1 egg, lightly beaten
1 drop oregano essential oil
1 drop basil essential oil
½ teaspoon each salt & pepper
2 tablespoons olive or vegetable oil
1 medium onion, peeled and diced
2 medium cloves garlic, peeled and minced
1 bell pepper, remove stem, ribs & seeds, diced
32 ounces vegetable stock
32 ounces beef stock
3 tablespoons tomato paste
½ cup orzo pasta
1 drop black pepper essential oil
1 drop oregano essential oil
1 drop lemon essential oil
Salt & Pepper

SERVES 4 - 6

Make the meatballs. In a bowl, mix beef, bread crumbs, egg, oregano EO, basil EO, and salt & pepper gently by hand. Roll mixture into 16 meatballs. Set aside.

Heat a large soup pan or Dutch oven atop the stove at medium heat. Once the pan is hot, add the oil. Once oil is hot, add the onion, garlic and bell peppers. Cook stirring often for 5 minutes.

continued

Add all stock, tomato paste, pasta and EO's. Bring to a soft boil, and gently add the meatballs.

After 4 to 5 minutes, stir carefully so the meatballs don't break apart. Reduce heat to low and simmer for one hour.

EO BENEFIT: Black pepper EO may be helpful for fatigue.

HINT: Mixing the meatball mixture gently by hand will help to keep the meatballs tender.

OPTIONAL SERVING IDEA: Garnish with 2 tablespoons chopped parsley and fresh Parmesan cheese.

MOROCCAN STYLE FISH SOUP

1 ½ pounds fresh fish (ex: swordfish, halibut, sea bass, grouper, or mahi mahi), skin and bones removed, cut into 2" cubes
1 small yellow or white onion, peeled and diced
1 celery stalk with the greens, sliced
3 medium garlic cloves, peeled and minced
2 tablespoons extra virgin olive or vegetable oil
1 red chili pepper, seeded and chopped (use as hot a pepper as you would like)
1 large potato, chopped (peeled or unpeeled)
16 ounces fish stock
2 medium tomatoes, chopped
1 drop cumin essential oil
1 drop cinnamon essential oil
1 drop coriander essential oil
2 drops lemon essential oil
2 drops dill essential oil
2 tablespoons chopped parsley

SERVES 4 - 6

Heat a Dutch oven or large soup pan over medium heat; once hot, add oil. Once oil is hot, add onions and celery - season with salt and pepper. Saute until vegetables are softened about 5 minutes. Add garlic and chili pepper; cooking and stirring another 3 minutes.

Add potatoes and cook for 3 more minutes.

continued

Add the stock. Cook until potatoes are fork tender (about 20 – 30 minutes).

Reduce heat to low, and add the fish and parsley, cook until the fish is cooked through (about 10 minutes).

Remove from heat and stir in EO's.

EO BENEFIT: Cinnamon EO may be good for joint pain.

HINT: If fresh fish is not available, use frozen fish; defrost before cutting into cubes.

OPTIONAL SERVING IDEA: Instead of adding cubed potatoes, use 2 cups mashed potatoes, which will thicken the soup to a chowder consistency.

CHICKEN WILD RICE SOUP

3 tablespoons olive oil or vegetable oil
3 tablespoons butter
½ a medium onion, peeled and finely diced
1 stalk celery with greens, finely diced
½ cup flour
3 cups chicken stock, heated for a minute in the microwave
¼ teaspoon garlic powder
½ teaspoon onion powder
1/2 teaspoon salt
½ teaspoon ground black pepper
3 cups cooked chicken, shredded (ex: from a
         rotisserie chicken)
3 cups cooked wild rice (cook according to package
         instructions replacing water with chicken stock)
¾ cups carrots, peeled and shredded
2 tablespoons sherry wine
1 cup heavy cream
¼ cup slivered almonds
5 drops thyme essential oil
3 drops celery seed essential oil
2 drops black pepper essential oil

SERVES 4 - 6

Heat a Dutch oven or large soup pan over medium heat. Once hot, add oil and butter; once hot, add onion and celery. Sautee until tender (about 5 minutes). Stir in flour until well blended (cook 1 minute) and gradually add the heated chicken stock, stirring to thicken. Add the garlic powder and onion powder; bring to a soft boil.

continued

Chicken Wild Rice Soup (continued)

Reduce heat to simmer. Stir in chicken, rice, and carrots and cook for 5 minutes. Stir in sherry, heavy cream and almonds. Simmer for 30 minutes to 1 hour.

Prior to serving, mix in EO's. Add salt and pepper to taste.

EO BENEFIT: Thyme EO may be helpful to boost the immune system.

HINT: For extra flavor, add 1 tablespoon concentrated bouillon (cube or paste) (ex: Better Than Boullion®)

TORTELLINI SOUP

2 tablespoons olive oil or vegetable oil
4 carrots, peeled and sliced into rounds
1 medium yellow or white onion, peeled and diced
2 stalks celery with greens, sliced
4 cloves garlic, peeled and minced
3 medium tomatoes, chopped
32 ounces vegetable stock
1 package cheese tortellini
4 cups spinach, chopped (about 4 good handfuls)
1 drop basil essential oil
1 drop rosemary essential oil
1 drop thyme essential oil
1 drop lemon essential oil

SERVES 4

Heat a Dutch oven or large soup pan over medium heat; add oil. Once the oil is hot, add carrots, onion, and celery; season with salt and pepper. Cook, stirring, for 3 minutes. Add garlic and tomatoes; saute another minute.
Add stock; bring to a low boil for 10 minutes.

Add tortellini and cook 2 minutes less than package instructions.

Remove from heat, stir in spinach and EO's. Gently stir well. Serve hot.

EO BENEFIT: Rosemary EO may be helpful to reduce inflammation.

SANDWICHES

ITALIAN STYLE TURKEY SUB

2 cloves garlic, peeled
5 basil leaves
1 drop basil essential oil
1 drop lemon essential oil
1 drop oregano essential oil
¼ cup olive oil
2 tablespoons red wine vinegar
Salt and pepper
1 loaf of Italian bread
1 pound sliced deli turkey breast
1 large tomato, sliced
2 cups shredded iceberg lettuce
½ small red onion, peeled and thinly sliced
Dill pickle slices
½ a red bell pepper (ribs removed and seeded),
     cut into very thin strips
2 tablespoons sliced black olives, drained
4 slices provolone cheese

SERVES 4

In a blender or food processor, puree garlic cloves, basil, EO's, olive oil, vinegar, and salt and pepper.

Slice bread into 4 equal servings then slice each piece lengthwise into a hoagie. Spread the garlic-basil mixture on one side of the bread.

Layer turkey, vegetables, and cheese on the bread.

EO BENEFIT: Oregano EO may be helpful for menstrual cramps.

GRILLED CHEESE WITH APPLE & BRIE & CHEDDAR

For each sandwich:
2 tablespoons butter, softened
1 drop rosemary essential oil
2 slices of bread (preferably, thick cut peasant style)
¼ Granny Smith apple, thinly sliced
2 – 4 slices of Brie cheese
1 slice extra sharp cheddar cheese
Additional butter

SERVES 1

Mix rosemary essential oil with butter. Spread evenly on one side of each of the bread slices.

Heat a large, non-stick skillet on medium heat. Place one slice of bread butter side down, layer with apples and cheeses. Place final slice of bread butter side up. Cook until toasty and browned; flip over and cook the other side until toasty brown.

EO BENEFIT: Rosemary EO may be helpful for headaches.

CHICKEN GYRO

For each gyro:
2 tablespoons plain Greek yogurt
1 drop lemon essential oil
1 drop dill essential oil
1 drop oregano essential oil
One pita bread, top removed to create a pocket
¼ pound cooked chicken breast, cut into thin slices
Cucumber, 5 to 6 thin slices (peel if desired)
Red onion, 5 to 6 thin slices (less or more as desired)
Tomato, 2 tablespoons diced

SERVES 1

Mix yogurt, essential oils, and vegetables together.

Heat a large skillet on medium low. Once hot, heat pita bread on each side until warm, around 3 minutes. Or, microwave on high for 8 seconds.

Spoon the chicken and vegetables into the warm pita bread with yogurt EO sauce on the side for dipping.

EO BENEFIT: Dill EO may be helpful for intestinal gas.

OPTIONAL SERVING IDEA: Replace pita bread with a tortilla for a wrap.

GRILLED ASPARAGUS HERO

Aioli:
4 large pieces of roasted red pepper (purchase in a jar)
2 tablespoons of oil from the roasted red pepper jar
1 medium sized garlic clove, peeled
1 drop oregano essential oil
1 drop lemon essential oil
2 tablespoons olive oil

Filling:
2 tablespoons olive oil
1 bunch asparagus, cleaned and stems removed,
     lightly salted

4 hoagie rolls, sliced lengthwise
4 slices mild white cheese (ex: American, Provolone)
Salt & pepper

SERVES 4

In a blender or food processor, puree pepper, pepper oil, garlic, EO's and 2 tablespoons of olive oil. Season with salt & pepper. Add olive oil slowly so that the aioli isn't too thin. Set aside.

In a large skillet on medium heat, heat 2 tablespoons olive oil, add asparagus and cook for 4 - 6 minutes (or longer, to your desired tenderness). Season with salt and pepper.

Spread aioli on one side of the rolls, top with asparagus and cheese.

continued

Grilled Asparagus Hero (continued)

Top with the other side of the roll and serve. If desired, place the cheese topped side of sandwich under the broiler to melt the cheese, then top with the other side of the roll and serve.

EO BENEFIT: Lemon EO may be helpful for mood elevation.

TEX-MEX CHICKEN-AVOCADO SANDWICH

2 slices bread (your choice)
¼ pound sliced deli fried chicken
½ avocado, peel and pit removed
1 tablespoon mayonnaise
1 drop cilantro essential oil
1 drop cumin essential oil
1 drop lime essential oil
1 slice pepper-jack cheese

SERVES 1

Mash avocado, mayonnaise, and EO's together. Spread on one piece of bread. Layer chicken and cheese atop avocado mixture and top with the other slice of bread.

EO BENEFIT: Cilantro EO may be helpful for balancing blood sugar.

HINT: Deli chicken can be replaced with leftover cooked chicken or rotisserie chicken

VEGETABLE SUBS

1 red bell pepper, ribs & seeds removed,
     sliced into thin strips
1 yellow bell pepper, ribs & seeds removed,
     sliced into thin strips
1 medium onion, peeled, halved, and thinly sliced
1 large portabella mushroom cap, sliced into thin strips
1 clove garlic, peeled and minced
1 drop oregano essential oil
1 drop basil essential oil
1 drop black pepper essential oil
2 tablespoons olive oil
2 tablespoons red wine vinegar
4 submarine rolls
Provolone cheese (optional)

SERVES 4

Mix all ingredients (except rolls and cheese) in a large plastic bag and marinate for 1 - 2 hours.

Heat a large skillet over medium high, pour vegetable contents (including marinade) into the pan and cook until tender (about 10 minutes).

Serve vegetables hot on the rolls. Top with cheese if desired.

EO BENEFIT: Oregano EO may be helpful for respiratory problems.

HINT: Gently wash mushrooms with a wet paper towel.

FISH TACOS

2 drops lime essential oil
1 drop cumin essential oil
1 teaspoon chili powder
Few dashes up to 1/8 teaspoon ground cayenne powder
Salt & pepper
1 pound of fish filets (ex: snapper, mahi mahi, grouper,
    halibut, or cod), skin and bones removed,
    cut into 2" pieces

Sauce:
1 cup plain Greek style yogurt
1 drop lime essential oil
2 drops cilantro essential oil

2 tablespoons olive oil
8 soft flour or corn tortillas (heated as per package instructions)
1 small tomato, seeds removed and minced
2 tablespoon red onion, peeled and minced

SERVES 4

Mix lime and cumin EO's, chili and cayenne powders, salt and pepper - rub onto the fish pieces.

Mix yogurt and lime & cilantro essential oils. Set aside.

Heat a skillet on medium high heat, add oil - when oil is hot, add the fish and cook until cooked through (about 4 minutes depending on the thickness of the fish).

continued

Fish Tacos (continued)

Evenly divide fish among tortillas top with yogurt sauce and garnish with chopped tomato and onion.

EO BENEFIT: Lime EO may be helpful for mental clarity.

HINT: Garnish with a wedge of fresh lime.

ROAST BEEF & ROASTED PEPPER
OREGANO MAYO PINWHEELS

Sauce:
½ jar roasted peppers, drained and minced
1/3 cup mayonnaise
3 drops oregano essential oil

4 wraps (purchase wraps of your choice)
1 pound deli roast beef, thinly cut
4 slices provolone cheese

Serves 4 - 6

Make the mayo: mix together roasted peppers, mayonnaise, EO.

Spread each wrap with the mayo mixture, layer roast beef and cheese atop. Then roll into a warp. Cut into pinwheel rounds.

EO BENEFIT: Oregano EO may be helpful for allergies.

HINT: Use a sharp knife to cut the pinwheel pieces.

OPTIONAL SERVING IDEA: Serve as an appetizer.

OPEN FACED CAPRESE SANDWICH

2 French bread rolls or 4 slices Artisan bread
2 Roma tomatoes, sliced lengthwise
1/2 pound fresh mozzarella, sliced
2 tablespoons extra virgin olive oil
2 tablespoons balsamic vinegar
1 to 2 drops basil essential oil
1 tablespoon minced fresh basil

Serves 2

Layer tomatoes and mozzarella on the bread.

Mix olive oil, vinegar, and EO together; drizzle atop sandwiches. Garnish with fresh basil

EO BENEFIT: Basil EO may be helpful for gout.

HINT: When tomatoes are in season, beef steak tomatoes are a delicious alternative to Roma tomatoes.

GRILLED HAM & CHEESE
WITH BLACK PEPPER DIJON MUSTARD

Sauce:
1 ½ tablespoons Dijon mustard
2 drops black pepper essential oil

2 thick slices of Artisan bread
2 tablespoons butter, softened
One tablespoon olive oil
¼ pound deli ham
1 slice Havarti cheese

SERVES 1

Heat a large skillet over medium heat.

Spread each slice of bread with butter on one side of the bread.

Mix the mustard and EO.

When the skillet is hot, add the olive oil.

Place one slice of bread, butter side down, into the pan. Top with ham and cheese.

On the unbuttered side of the other piece of bread, spread the mustard mixture. Then, place it on the sandwich butter side up. Let the sandwich cook until toasted - then carefully flip to toast the other side. Gently press on the bread and cook until nicely toasted on the other side.

continued

Grilled Ham & Cheese (continued)

EO BENEFIT: Black pepper EO may be helpful in relieving aches and pains.

HINT: Delicious use for leftover holiday ham.

OPTIONAL SERVING IDEA: Serve with melon wedges.

SAUSAGE SLIDERS

Sausage:
1 pound ground pork
1 drop fennel essential oil
1 drop oregano essential oil
1 drop basil essential oil
2 drops black pepper essential oil
1 tablespoon fresh parsley, chopped
½ teaspoon garlic powder
½ teaspoon onion powder
2 tablespoons tomato paste
1 tablespoon red wine vinegar
Salt

2 tablespoons olive or vegetable oil

8 slider buns
4 pieces of provolone or mozzarella cheese, halved
2 tablespoons water

Make the sausage by gently mixing the ingredients by hand in a bowl. Refrigerate at least an hour or overnight.

Form the sausage mixture into 8 small patties.

Heat a large skillet on medium heat; once hot, add the oil. Once the oil is hot, cook the patties 4 minutes on each side until cooked through. Place cheese atop the patties, add 2 tablespoons water to the pan; cover the pan and cook until the cheese is melted.

Place cooked sliders onto the buns.

continued

Sausage Sliders (continued)

SERVES 4

EO BENEFIT: Oregano essential oil may be helpful for rheumatism.

HINT: Spread one side of the bread with Dijon or Spicy Brown mustard.

OPTIONAL SERVING IDEA: Replace slider buns with King's Hawaiian® Sweet Rolls.

MAIN ENTREES

LEMON-DILL SHRIMP WITH BEANS

2 tablespoons olive oil
½ pound medium sized shrimp, shelled and deveined
7 ½ ounces of canned white beans (ex: Navy beans)
2 tablespoons butter
3 drops lemon essential oil
1 drop dill essential oil
2 drops black pepper essential oil
1 tablespoons capers, drained
Fresh dill leaves for garnish

SERVES 2

Heat a medium sized skillet on medium high. When the pan is hot, add the olive oil – swirl it around so the bottom of the pan is mostly coated. Add the shrimp until cooked through (no longer translucent).

Reduce heat to low, add the beans and cook until beans are hot (about 2 minutes)

Remove from the heat, add butter, essential oils, and capers. Stir well. Serve hot, garnished with fresh dill.

continued

Lemon-Dill Shrimp with Beans (continued)

EO BENEFIT: Lemon essential oil may be helpful for blood circulation.

HINT: Frozen shrimp can be used in place of fresh shrimp; defrost and pat dry before cooking.

OPTIONAL SERVING IDEA: Mix in 2 Roma tomatoes chopped.

FISH FINGERS WITH HOMEMADE TARTAR SAUCE

Sauce:
1 dill pickle spear, minced
½ cup mayonnaise
1 tablespoon capers, mashed
4 drops lemon essential oil

¾ pound firm white fish (ex: grouper, halibut, snapper),
      skin and bones removed, cut into 2" thick pieces
1 egg
1 tablespoon water
¾ cup Panko bread crumbs
¼ cup olive oil
Salt

SERVES 3 - 4

Make the tartar sauce by combining the pickle, mayonnaise, capers and EO together. Set aside.

Rinse the fish and pat dry. Cut fish into even sized "fingers".

Beat the egg with 1 tablespoon water. Dredge the fish pieces in the egg mixture, then coat with bread crumbs. After all pieces of fish are coated in bread crumbs, heat a large skillet on medium heat. When the pan is hot, add 2 tablespoons of the oil; once the oil is hot add the coated fish to the pan. Cook until nicely browned on all sides and cooked through (about 8 minutes). Season with salt.

.

continued

Fish Fingers with Homemade Tartar Sauce (continued)

Serve cooked fish with tartar sauce.

EO BENEFIT: Lemon essential oil may be helpful for anxiety.

HINT: Cook the fish in batches and do not overcrowd the pan. Add more oil between batches if necessary.

OPTIONAL SERVING IDEA: Cut fish into bite sized chunks and serve as an appetizer.

STEAK WITH CHIMICHURRI SAUCE

Sauce:
1/3 cup red wine vinegar
½ cup olive oil
1 teaspoon kosher salt
3 - 4 cloves garlic, minced
1 shallot, minced
½ cup chopped parsley
¼ cup chopped cilantro
1 drop oregano essential oil
2 drops lemon essential oil
2 drops black pepper essential oil

1 ½ pounds flank or skirt steak
¼ olive oil
Salt & pepper

SERVES 4

Make the sauce by pureeing all ingredients in a blender or food processor. Let set for at least an hour.

Cut the steak into equal sized serving portions.

Heat your grill or grill pan until hot. Brush both sides of the steak with olive oil and season with salt and pepper.

Grill 3 minutes each side for medium rare (preferred temperature) or cook to the doneness you prefer.
Let the steak rest 5 minutes before slicing against the grain.
Serve sliced steak topped with chimichurri sauce.

continued

Steak with Chimichurri Sauce (continued)

EO BENEFIT: Oregano EO may be helpful for a sore throat.

HINT: The chimichurri sauce can be made up to a week ahead and stored in the refrigerator. Leftover sauce can be stored the same way. Note that after a day, the herbs may become darkened and discolored – the sauce is still safe to eat. Bring up to remove temperature to serve.

OPTIONAL SERVING IDEA: Add another 2 tablespoons of olive oil to the sauce and toss it with cooked pasta. Serve the steak atop the pasta.

PORK & RADISH LETTUCE WRAPS

1 head bibb lettuce (aka Boston bibb, Boston, Butter)
1 pound ground pork
2 tablespoons olive oil (or other vegetable cooking oil)
1 small onion, peeled & minced
½ a bell pepper, stem, seed & ribs removed, minced
2 tablespoons soy sauce
1/8 teaspoon sesame oil
1 bunch radishes, cleaned and diced (if in good condition,
          chop 2 tablespoons of radish greens for garnish)
1 teaspoon toasted sesame seeds
2 drops lime essential oil
1 drop cilantro essential oil
2 drops lemon essential oil
1 drop basil essential oil
1 drop ginger essential oil or ¼ teaspoon ground ginger

SERVES 4

Prepare the bibb lettuce. Carefully remove each leaf, gently
rinse under cold water and pat try. Set aside.

Heat a good sized skillet over medium high heat, add the oil,
once the oil is hot, add the pork, onion, and pepper. Saute until
the pork is cooked through about 8 minutes.

Remove from heat, stir in the soy sauce and sesame oil, diced
radishes, sesame seeds, and EOs. Mix well.

Evenly divide the pork mixture among the lettuce "cups" and
garnish with radish greens.

continued

Pork & Radish Lettuce Wraps (continued)

EO BENEFIT: Ginger essential oil may help digestive issues.

HINT: Romaine or iceberg lettuce can replace the bibb lettuce.

OPTIONAL SERVING IDEA: Tear the lettuce into pieces and spoon the pork mixture over the lettuce.

LEMON GARLIC CHICKEN
WITH FRESH PARSLEY-ALMOND PESTO

1 cup flat parsley leaves
¼ cup slivered almonds, lightly toasted
¾ cup avocado oil (or extra virgin olive oil)
4 drops lemon essential oil
2 drops black pepper essential oil
1 teaspoon salt
¼ cup flour seasoned with salt & pepper
¼ cup avocado oil (or extra virgin olive oil)
          (use 2 tablespoons at a time)
1 pound boneless, skinless chicken breasts
1 cup chicken stock
5 large cloves garlic, peeled and cut into slivers
Zest (in strips) from 1 lemon (reserve the lemon
          for another use)

SERVES 4

In a heavy skillet over medium high heat, add 2 tablespoons of the oil. Dredge the chicken pieces in the flour and carefully place into the pan. Brown on both sides. Remove from the pan.

Add the stock to the pan ("deglaze") – stir to loosen the flavor pieces stuck to the bottom of the pan. Turn the heat to medium – let the stock simmer. Add the garlic and ½ lemon strips to the pan. Add the chicken and any accumulated juices back into the pan and let simmer 8 – 10 minutes until the chicken is cooked through.

continued

Lemon Garlic Chicken (continued)

Depending on the thickness of the breasts, you may need to cook a little longer - internal temperature should be 165 degrees.

Remove the cooked chicken from the pan to a new plate and cover with foil to keep warm. Continue cooking the sauce over medium low heat (stirring often) until reduced.

In a food processor or blender, pulse the parsley, almonds, avocado oil, EO's and salt.

Serve with broth spooned over the top of the chicken and top it with a dollop of the pesto.

EO BENEFIT: Lemon essential oil may aid the circulatory system and hypertension.

LAMB PATTIES WITH YOGURT SAUCE

Sauce:
3 tablespoons olive oil
1 tablespoon feta cheese
1 cup Greek yogurt
1 drop basil essential oil
1 drop oregano essential oil
1 drop lemon essential oil
Salt

Patties:
1 pound ground lamb
1 large egg, lightly beaten
1 tablespoon onion, minced
1 teaspoon fresh basil, minced
1 drop oregano essential oil
2 drops black pepper essential oil
1 drop coriander essential oil

1 - 2 tablespoons olive oil

SERVES 4

Make the sauce. Mix all the ingredients in a blender or food processor. Set aside.

Make the patties. Gently, by hand, mix the patty ingredients in a bowl for about a minute. Section into 4 equal portions and form into patties. Coat both sides of each patty with olive oil

continued

121

Lamb Patties with Yogurt Sauce (continued)

Heat a grill, skillet, or grill pan to medium high heat. Cook 4-5 minutes on each side for medium (cook to desired temperature).

Serve the cooked patties topped with the yogurt sauce

EO BENEFIT: Coriander EO may be helpful for diabetes.

HINT: Serve garnished with Kalamata olives and sliced cucumbers.

OPTIONAL SERVING IDEA: Serve on toasted Kaiser rolls.

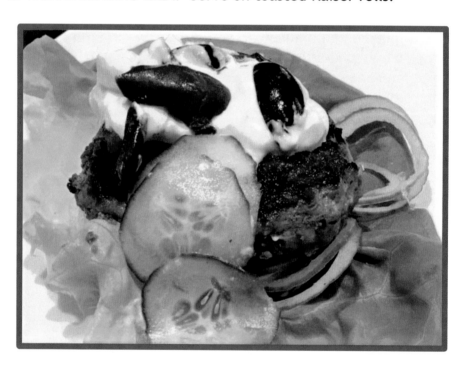

THAI STYLED SALMON WITH CUCUMBER SALAD

Cucumber salad:
1 English (aka Hothouse, seedless) cucumber –
     sliced very thin
3 green onions (aka scallions) – sliced
     (both white and green sections)
1 small bell pepper, stem, ribs & seeds removed,
     diced small
1/3 of a small red onion, peeled & minced
1 tablespoon salt
2 tablespoons sugar
½ cup rice wine vinegar
½ teaspoon sesame seeds
1/8 teaspoon sesame oil
1 drop black pepper essential oil
1 drop cilantro essential oil
1 drop lime essential oil
1 drop tangerine essential oil

Salmon:
1 ½ pounds quality salmon fillets with the skin on
     cut to size to fit into the pan
2 tablespoons reduced sodium soy sauce
1 tablespoon pure maple sugar
2 tablespoons Thai chili paste
Juice of a lime
3 tablespoons olive oil

SERVES 4

continued

Thai Styled Salmon with Cucumber Salad (continued)

Mix the salad ingredients in a large bowl. Cover and set in the fridge for at least an hour and up to four hours. Stir the mixture at least once every half hour so that all the vegetables get pickled.

Five minutes prior to cooking the salmon, remove the fish from the fridge. Rinse and pat the fillets dry.

In a small bowl, mix the soy sauce, maple syrup, chili paste, and lime juice. Gently smear the mixture on top of the salmon.

Preheat a large skillet on medium high until hot. Once the oil is hot, place the salmon in the pan skin side down and cook to your desired temperature. Depending on the thickness of the fish, this can take from 7 - 12 minutes.

Serve the cooked salmon with the cucumber salad.

continued

Thai Styled Salmon with Cucumber Salad (continued)

EO BENEFIT: Cilantro EO may be helpful as a natural detoxifier.

HINT: If fresh salmon fillets are not available, frozen salmon is a good alternative. Defrost the salmon prior to cooking.

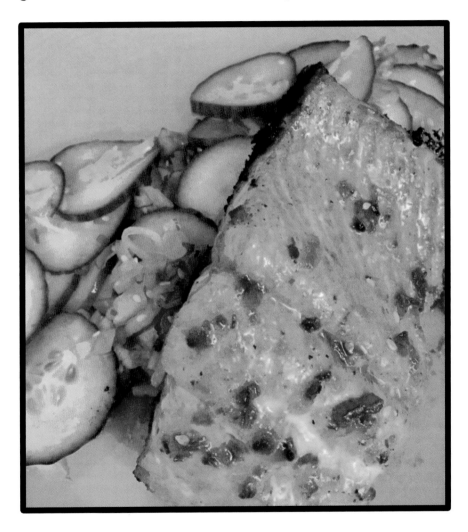

TUNA BITES POACHED IN OLIVE OIL

1 pound tuna (ex: Ahi) steaks, cut into 2" cubes
2 cups olive oil
1 sprig of rosemary
2 large garlic cloves, skinned and "smashed"
1/8 teaspoon red pepper flakes (or more to your taste)
2 drops lemon essential oil
2 drops grapefruit essential oil
1 drop black pepper essential oil

SERVES 4

Remove tuna from the refrigerator. In a large deep skillet heat all ingredients except tuna cubes on low heat for 30 minutes to infuse all flavors into the oil.

Bring the pan up to medium heat (garlic will begin to sizzle) and add tuna cubes. Spoon hot oil over the tuna for 5 to 6 minutes – The fish will be medium to medium rare; adjust time to cook to your desired temperature.

EO BENEFIT: Grapefruit EO may be helpful for anxiety.

HINT: To discard the oil, wait until it has cooled, then carefully dump it into a zipper plastic bag and discard.

OPTIONAL SERVING IDEA: Serve with Grapefruit and Fennel Cucumber Cups on page 17

CHICKEN SATAY WITH PEANUT DIPPING SAUCE

Skewers:
1 pound chicken tenders (or 1 pound chicken breast
        cut into tender sized strips)
¼ cup olive oil
2 tablespoons raw apple cider vinegar
Juice of half a lemon
1/8 teaspoon ground cayenne powder
1 tablespoon fresh ginger, grated
2 medium cloves of garlic, minced
2 drops black pepper essential oil
2 drops lemon essential oil
¼ cup fresh parsley, minced
1 teaspoon agave nectar or local honey

Sauce:
½ cup creamy peanut butter
2 tablespoons warm water
2 tablespoons reduced sodium soy sauce
Juice of half a lime
1/8 teaspoon cayenne powder
1 tablespoon molasses
1 drop cilantro essential oil

SERVES 4

Make the skewers. Put the chicken onto skewers and place into a glass dish or plastic zipper bag (do not pierce the bag). Mix all the other ingredients (set aside 3 tablespoons) and pour over the chicken. Let marinate in the refrigerator at least one hour and up to 4 hours.

continued

Make the sauce. Blend all sauce ingredients in a blender or food processor until smooth. If sauce is overly thick, add one teaspoon of warm water at a time, stirring to get to desired consistency.

Cook the skewers. Remove chicken from the marinade and discard the marinade. Cook on the grill, under the broiler, or in a hot skillet until chicken is cooked through (depending on thickness, about 8 minutes). Season the cooked skewers with salt and pepper.

Serve the skewers with dipping sauce.

EO BENEFIT: Lemon EO may be helpful for urinary tract infections.

HINT: Dipping sauce can be made ahead and stored in the refrigerator in an airtight container up to a week – bring to room temperature and mix before serving.

BUTTERNUT SQUASH - QUINOA BOWL

2 pounds butternut squash, peeled, seeded, and chopped
     into 1" chunks (or 10 ounces frozen – defrosted)
1 small onion, peeled, halved and sliced thin
½ red bell pepper, stem, ribs & seeds removed, diced
1 stalk celery with greens, thinly sliced
1 clove garlic, peeled and minced
2 tablespoons olive oil
Salt & pepper
1 ½ cups quinoa (cooked as per package instructions, but
     replace the water with vegetable stock
2 cups fresh spinach
¼ cup pistachio nuts, shelled (roasted or raw)
¼ cup pomegranate flavored dried cranberries or
     pomegranate seeds
1 tablespoon paprika
½ cup vegetable stock
1 tablespoon honey
1 drops thyme essential oil
1 drop black pepper essential oil
1 drop lemon essential oil
Salt & pepper

Preheat oven to 400 degrees. On a rimmed baking sheet, spread
squash chunks into a single layer. Bake until they are fork
tender (about 20 minutes).

Heat a large skillet over medium heat, when hot, add olive oil
and heat. Add the onion, pepper, celery and garlic with salt &
pepper and cook until softened – about 6 minutes. This can be
done and set aside until the squash is cooked.

continued

Butternut Squash – Quinoa Bowl (continued)

Over medium low heat, add all ingredients and gently stir to coat.

EO BENEFIT: Thyme EO may be helpful for cardiovascular issues.

HINT: Chopping the spinach before adding it to the pan will allow it to be more evenly dispersed.

OPTIONAL SERVING IDEA: Replace cooked quinoa with cooked lentils.

SUN DRIED TOMATO SHRIMP

4 tablespoons oil from tomato jar (see ingredient below)
2 cups of fresh baguette bread, cut into small cubes
2 tablespoons finely chopped fresh parsley
1 pound medium sized shrimp, shelled and deveined
2 tablespoons olive oil
15 ounce can of cannellini beans
7 - 9 ounces sun dried tomatoes (purchased in a jar, packed
     in oil), chop julienne style (reserve 4 tablespoons of
     the oil - see above and below)
1 drop oregano essential oil
2 tablespoons capers plus 2 tablespoons of the caper brine

SERVES 4

In a medium skillet, heat the 4 tablespoons of sundried tomato oil on medium heat until almost smoking. Add the bread cubes and cook (stirring) until the bread is toasted. Remove from heat; stir in the parsley. Set aside.

Heat a medium sized skillet on medium high. When the pan is hot, add the olive oil - swirl it around so the bottom of the pan is mostly coated and reduce the heat to medium. Add the shrimp until cooked through - no longer translucent.

Reduce heat to low, add the beans and cook until beans are hot (about 2 minutes)

continued

131

Sun Dried Tomato Shrimp (continued)

Remove from the heat, and stir in sun dried tomatoes, EO's, and capers with brine. Stir well. Serve hot garnished with toasted bread cubes.

EO BENEFIT: Oregano EO may be helpful for arthritis

HINT: Use the same pan you used to toast the bread to cook the shrimp.

OPTIONAL SERVING IDEA: Serve over a bed of greens.

MUSTARD SWISS PORK CHOPS

4 boneless loin pork chops, 5 – 6 ounces each
¼ cup Dijon mustard
1 drop rosemary essential oil
1 tablespoon balsamic vinegar
¼ cup sour cream or plain Greek yogurt
4 slices Swiss cheese

SERVES 4

Preheat oven to 350. Spray pan with no stick spray or spread some olive oil on the pan. Place pork chops in pan.
Mix mustard, essential oil, balsamic vinegar and sour cream/yogurt. Spoon the mixture over the pork chops.

Bake for 20 minutes. Place a slice of Swiss cheese on each chop, and bake for another 10 minutes.

EO BENEFIT: Rosemary EO may be helpful for mental concentration.

HINT: Trim extra fat from the pork chop before putting it into the pan.

OPTIONAL SERVING IDEA: Serve with a side of Orange-Rosemary carrots from page 156.

SPINACH PESTO PASTA

3 cups fresh spinach leaves (3 large handfuls)
½ cup olive oil
2 large cloves garlic, peeled and smashed
2 tablespoons pine nuts (separated)
2 drops basil essential oil
4 drops lemon essential oil
2 ounces shredded freshly grated parmesan cheese
    (plus more for garnish)
4 servings cooked pasta (hot or cold)

SERVES 4

Puree all ingredients (except 1 tablespoon of the pine nuts and the pasta) in a blender or food processor.

Toss the pasta with the pesto and garnish with 1 tablespoon pine nuts.

EO BENEFIT: Basil EO may be helpful for inflammation.

BEET RAVIOLI WITH
BEET GREENS AND GOAT CHEESE SAUCE

4 medium sized red or golden beets (greens included)
4 large cloves garlic
1 tablespoon olive oil
1 package wonton wrappers
½ cup ricotta cheese
2 tablespoons unseasoned bread crumbs
2 tablespoons olive oil
4 ounces goat cheese (aka chevre)
2 cups heavy or whipping cream
2 drops lemon essential oil
Salt & pepper

SERVES 4

Preheat oven to 400 degrees. Separate the beets from the beet greens. Rinse all well. Set greens aside. Wrap each beet in aluminum foil and place onto a rimmed baking sheet. Wrap the garlic cloves into one piece of foil, pour olive oil atop, wrap tightly, and add to baking sheet. Cook until beets are tender (pierce with a fork or knife to test) - about 45 minutes. Remove from the oven, carefully unwrap the foil, and allow to cool.

Once the beets are cool to the touch, peel and grate into a bowl. Mix in ricotta cheese & bread crumbs.

Chill a rimmed baking sheet. If it doesn't fit into your refrigerator or freezer, put a plastic bag of ice on the pan for 5 minutes (wipe off any moisture).

continued

Beet Ravioli (continued)

One wonton at a time, take a wrapper and fill with a scoop of the beet mixture, wet all edges of the wrapper edge, top with another wonton wrapper. Press out all air and seal the ravioli. Place on the chilled tray.

Once all ravioli are prepared, set aside. Add water to a medium sized pot, add 2 tablespoons salt, bring to a boil, then reduce heat to bring to a strong simmer.

Coarsely chop the beet greens. Heat a large skillet on medium high heat, once hot, add 2 tablespoons olive oil. Once the oil is hot, add the beet greens. Sautee until softened – about 8 minutes. Reduce heat to low – add the milk and goat cheese, stirring until softened. Add the roasted garlic by squeezing it out of its skin, and stir well. Hold at a low temperature stirring frequently.

Cook the ravioli by adding to the simmering water. Do not crowd the pan, cook in batches if needed. Cook 2 – 3 minutes; using a slotted spoon, move the cooked ravioli into the skillet.

Once all ravioli are in the skillet, add lemon EO and gently stir or toss to evenly coat the ravioli with sauce. Serve hot.

EO BENEFIT: Lemon EO may be helpful for digestion issues.

HINT: Beet juice can stain your clothes. Use caution when handling them.

SIDE DISHES

BLEU BRUSSELS SPROUTS

1 pound brussels sprouts (wash, remove & discard
        outer leaves, cut sprouts into wedges)
1 medium shallot, peeled and minced
¼ pound thickly cut pancetta, diced
3 tablespoon bleu cheese crumbles (reserve 1 tablespoon
        for garnish)
1 tablespoon balsamic vinegar
4 drops lemon essential oil
3 drops black pepper essential oil

SERVES 4

In a large skillet over medium heat, cook the pancetta until
crispy. Use a slotted spoon to remove the pancetta and set
aside.

If the pancetta did not render much fat, add a tablespoon of
olive oil to the pan. Add the shallot and brussels sprouts to the
pan. Let the sprouts cook until slightly crispy before turning.
Cook until softened. Add a tablespoon of water to create a
steaming effect and stir well.

Remove from heat and stir in the 2 tablespoons bleu cheese
crumbles, balsamic vinegar, and EO's. Serve hot garnished with
pancetta and bleu cheese crumbles.

EO BENEFIT: Black pepper EO may be helpful for muscle aches.

HINT: You can substitute frozen brussels sprouts for fresh.
Defrost and drain before cutting into wedges and cooking.

BLISTERED CHERRY TOMATOES

1 pint cherry tomatoes
2 tablespoons olive or avocado oil
1 shallot, peeled and thinly sliced
2 drops basil essential oil
2 drops lemon essential oil
1 drop black pepper essential oil
2 tablespoons golden raisins
2 tablespoons pine nuts - toasted
Fresh basil - cut chiffonade style

SERVES 2 - 4

Heat a skillet on medium heat, add the olive oil. Once the oil is heated, add the shallot and cook for 3 minutes. Remove the shallots from the pan and set aside. Increase the heat to medium high, if the shallots absorbed most of the oil, add more oil. Put the tomatoes in the pan. Let them cook until blistered on a couple of sides about 5 minutes.

Remove from the heat, stir in shallots, EO's, raisins, pine nuts and salt. Garnish with fresh basil.

EO BENEFIT: Basil EO may be helpful for or low spirits.

SAUTEED BABY KALE

5 ounce package of Baby Kale
Small onion, peeled, halved and sliced
2 large garlic cloves, peeled and minced
2 tablespoons olive oil
2 drops coriander essential oil
2 drops fennel essential oil
Salt & pepper

SERVES 2

Heat a large skillet over medium low heat. Once hot, add the olive oil and heat. Add the onions and garlic. Saute until the onions and garlic start to soften, about 5 minutes. Add the kale and saute until cooked down to desired doneness.

Remove from heat; stir in EO's. Season with salt and pepper.

EO BENEFIT: Coriander essential oil may be helpful to soothe arthritis.

OPTIONAL SERVING IDEA: When cooking, mixing in 2 tablespoons of pine nuts.

RED CABBAGE, APPLE & ONION

2 tablespoons olive oil
1 small head red cabbage, cleaned and cut into shreds
2 tart apples (ex: Granny Smith), cored and cubed
1 small red onion, peeled and sliced into thin rounds
1/3 cup red wine vinegar
3 drops fennel essential oil
2 drops coriander essential oil
Salt & Pepper to taste
2 tablespoons slivered almonds (optional garnish)

SERVES 4

Heat a Dutch oven or large skillet with a cover on medium heat, add the olive oil, and stir in the cabbage, apples, and onion. Continue cooking on medium heat stirring often until the cabbage is wilted, the apples softened, and the onions translucent (about 10 minutes). Add the vinegar and essential oils – mix well.

EO BENEFIT: Fennel EO may be helpful for heart health.

SWEET POTATO HASH

2 medium sized sweet potatoes, peeled and cut into
      small cubes
1 yellow bell pepper, seeds, stem, and ribs discarded
1 red bell pepper, seeds, stem, and ribs discarded
White or yellow medium sized onion, peeled and
      finely diced
2 tablespoons olive oil
1 tablespoon paprika
1/8 teaspoon cayenne powder
2 drops cinnamon essential oil
2 drops nutmeg essential oil
1 drop black pepper essential oil

SERVES 4 - 6

Heat a large skillet on medium high heat, add olive oil - once
hot, add vegetables and dry seasonings. Cook for 2 minutes,
then reduce heat to medium. Cook until potatoes are softened
(about 10 minutes).

Remove from heat, stir in EO's. Salt and pepper to taste.

EO BENEFIT: Nutmeg EO may be helpful for neuropathy.

GRILLED CORN WITH CILANTRO LIME BUTTER

½ cup butter, softened
3 drops cilantro essential oil
2 drops lime essential oil
1 drop black pepper essential oil
1 teaspoon lime zest
10 ears sweet corn, husked and cleaned

SERVES 5 - 10

Mix butter, EO's, and lime zest together. Set aside.

Heat grill or a grill pan to medium, cook corn until it has light char marks and corn has softened (about 15 - 20 minutes)

Serve corn topped with flavored butter. Season with salt and pepper.

EO BENEFIT: Lime EO may improve the lymphatic system.

HINT: If cooking on a hot grill, a few minutes of direct heat will intensify the charring.

OPTIONAL SERVING IDEA: Slice the kernels from the cooked corn (let cool before cutting) and use as a garnish for nachos or tacos.

WILD RICE PILAF

1 cup wild rice, rinsed
4 cups vegetable stock
½ teaspoon salt
8 ounce package baby bella mushrooms, cleaned and
      thinly sliced
1 tablespoon butter
2 ounces slivered almonds
2 drops thyme essential oil
1 drop lemon essential oil
Salt & pepper to taste

SERVES 4

In a medium sauce pan, heat pan on medium high, add butter. Once butter has melted, and mushrooms and cook for 3 minutes. Add wild rice, vegetable stock, salt, and almonds - stir well. Bring to a boil, then reduce to simmer. Let simmer for 45 - 50 minutes until rice is tender.

Remove from heat and stir in essential oil and season with salt and pepper.

EO BENEFIT: Thyme EO may be helpful for infections (ex: common cold).

HINT: To clean mushrooms, rinse under cold water and quickly pat dry with paper towels.

OPTIONAL SERVING IDEA: Use as the basis for a "pilaf bowl" and add your choice of cooked protein and vegetables.

TARRAGON LEMON RISOTTO

¾ cup Arborio rice
2 tablespoons butter or olive oil
1 shallot, peeled and minced
3 cups vegetable stock
2 drops tarragon essential oil
3 drops lemon essential oil
Salt
Fresh tarragon for garnish

SERVES 4

Heat a medium sized sauce pan over medium heat; when hot, add the butter and melt it. Add the shallots and saute for 3 minutes.

Add the rice to the pan and "toast" it, stirring constantly for about 3 minutes (rice will very lightly brown). Reduce heat to medium low.

Add half a cup of stock at a time, stirring until the stock has absorbed (about 2 - 3 minutes each time). Once absorbed, add the next half a cup of stock. You are slow cooking the rice in the simmering liquid. This step should not be rushed or the risotto may become tough.

Cook until rice has softened and no longer has a "bite" to it.

Remove from heat, stir in EO's and season with salt. Garnish with tarragon.

continued

Tarragon Lemon Risotto (continued)

EO BENEFIT: Tarragon EO may be helpful for pre-menstrual syndrome.

HINT: If the stock is refrigerated, heat it in the microwave on high for 1 before adding to the rice.

OPTIONAL SERVING IDEA: Top with seared scallops and serve as an entrée.

ROASTED CAULIFLOWER

1 head cauliflower, cut into florets
2 large cloves garlic, peeled and thinly sliced
¼ olive oil (2 tablespoons reserved)
Salt & pepper
2 drops lemon essential oil
2 drops thyme essential oil

SERVES 4

Preheat oven to 450 degrees.

On a rimmed baking sheet, toss the cauliflower and garlic with olive oil (reserve 2 tablespoons).   Season with salt & pepper. Roast until golden, about 20 - 30 minutes.

Mix reserved 2 tablespoons of olive oil with essential oils; drizzle over the cooked cauliflower.

EO BENEFIT: Thyme EO may be helpful for memory issues.

CILANTRO LIME RICE

1 cup basmati or jasmine rice, rinsed
2 cups water
Juice of 1 lime
½ teaspoon salt
1 tablespoon butter
1 drop cilantro essential oil
1 drop lime essential oil
1 tablespoon fresh chopped cilantro (optional)

SERVES 4

Add rice, water, lime juice, salt and butter to a medium sized sauce pan. Over medium high heat, bring to a boil. Reduce heat to simmer, cover the pan and cook until tender (about 20 minutes).

Remove from heat, stir in EO's and chopped cilantro.

EO BENEFIT: Cilantro EO may be helpful for high blood sugar.

HINT: Use a rice steamer or instant pot in place of the stove top method. Follow the instructions for your appliance.

OPTIONAL SERVING IDEA: Use the cooked rice as a filling for tacos, quesadillas, or enchiladas.

KALE & CHARD

1 large bunch of kale <u>and</u> Swiss or Rainbow Chard –
    stems and ribs removed, chopped
¼ cup olive oil
2 large garlic cloves, peeled and cut into slivers
1 small onion, peeled and minced
1/2 cup vegetable stock
2 tablespoons red wine vinegar
2 drops lemon essential oil
2 drops black pepper essential oil

SERVES 3 – 4

Heat a large skillet over medium heat – add oil. Once the oil is hot, add garlic and onions. Cook for 2 minutes stirring regularly. Add the kale and chard.

Cook the kale and chard until softened – stir often – about 5 minutes. Turn the heat up to high and add the stock and vinegar. Cook – stirring frequently – for 10 minutes. Remove from heat and stir in the EO's. Serve hot.

EO BENEFIT: Black pepper EO may be helpful for tendonitis.

CHORIZO CORN BREAD DRESSING

4 tablespoons butter
2 tablespoons olive oil
1 large onion, peeled and minced
1 red bell pepper, seeds, stem and ribs removed, diced
2 large cloves garlic, peeled and minced
2 stalks celery (greens included), diced
1 pound chorizo sausage, chopped
1 8 ounce package cornbread cubes
2 - 3 cups vegetable stock
2 drops cumin essential oil
1 drop lemon essential oil
1 drop black pepper essential oil
Salt & Pepper

SERVES 4 - 6

Preheat oven to 350 degrees. Use the butter to grease a 9 x 13 glass casserole dish.

Place a medium sized skillet over medium heat, once hot, add olive oil. Once the oil is hot, add the onion, pepper, garlic, celery and chorizo. Sautee 8 minutes.

In a large bowl, combine the sautéed vegetables & chorizo with the cornbread cubes. Add 1 cup of the stock and stir; add more stock a ½ cup at a time until dressing reaches the desired consistency – moist but not mushy.

Stir in EO's; add salt & pepper. Pour into prepared dish.
Bake for 40 minutes and browned on top.

EO BENEFIT: Cumin EO may be helpful for water retention

·

GREEN BEANS WITH SLIVERED ALMONDS

2 tablespoons olive oil
1 pound fresh green beans, ends removed
1 tablespoon olive oil
1 large clove garlic, peeled and minced
1 medium shallot, peeled and sliced
¼ cup slivered almonds, toasted
2 tablespoons apple cider vinegar
2 drops coriander essential oil

SERVES 4

Place a large skillet over medium heat, once hot, add the 2 tablespoons oil. Once the oil is hot, add green beans – saute for 5 minutes. Add last tablespoon oil, garlic and shallot; saute for 5 minutes.

Stir in almonds. Add vinegar and stir well.

Remove from heat and add EO – stir well.

EO BENEFIT: Coriander EO may be have aphrodisiac qualities.

HINT: Cook the green beans to your decided tenderness, adding or reducing the cook time.

OPTIONAL SERVING IDEA: Add chopped country ham.

ROOT VEGETABLE GRATIN

4 tablespoons butter
3 cups heavy cream
3 large cloves garlic, peeled and minced
3 drops thyme essential oil
1 drop lemon essential oil
1 cup vegetable stock
2 tablespoons butter
1 tablespoon olive oil
1 ½ cups panko breadcrumbs
4 pounds assorted root vegetables (1 pound of each):
      potatoes, beets, turnip, rutabaga, celery root,
      parsnip, carrot, sweet potato, **or** yam
1 ½ cups grated parmesan cheese

Serves 6 - 8

Preheat oven to 400 degrees. Use the 4 tablespoons of butter to grease a 9 x 13 glass baking dish.

In a medium sized sauce pan over medium low heat, add heavy cream and garlic. Once hot (don't let it boil), turn heat to low and let simmer for 5 minutes. Remove from heat, let cool for 10 minutes then stir in EO's and vegetable stock.

Heat a medium sized skillet over medium heat; once hot, add the 2 tablespoons butter and olive oil. Once the butter has melted and is frothy, add the bread crumbs. Stir to toast the breadcrumbs until lightly browned.

continued

Remove breadcrumbs from heat and set aside in a bowl (remove from the pan to avoid over cooking).

Prepare the vegetables by peeling and thinly slicing. Rinse all vegetables in cold water. Pat dry with paper towels.

Evenly layer vegetables, cream mixture, and grated parmesan cheese into the buttered baking dish.

Cover dish with either foil or parchment paper. Cook for 40 minutes. Remove cover and top with bread crumbs. Cook an additional 10 minutes until the breadcrumbs are browned (watch carefully so the breadcrumbs do not burn).

EO BENEFIT: Thyme EO may be helpful in improving respiratory function.

HINT: Slicing the vegetables with a mandolin keeps the vegetables the same size, so they cook more evenly.

OPTIONAL SERVING IDEA: Between the layers of vegetables, mix in ground beef that has been browned and drained of extra fat.

ORANGE-ROSEMARY CARROTS

1 pound bag of baby cut carrots
1 cup orange juice
1 medium garlic clove, peeled and minced
1 tablespoon honey
2 dashes cayenne powder
1 drop rosemary essential oil
1 drop thyme essential oil

SERVES 4

Place carrots, orange juice, and garlic into a sauce pan on medium high heat. Bring to a boil, then reduce to low to simmer. Cook carrots to desired tenderness.

Remove from heat, stir in honey and EO's.

EO BENEFIT: Rosemary EO may be helpful for impaired memory.

HINT: If using whole carrots, peel and slice into 1 ½ to 2" pieces.

DESSERTS

BERRIES WITH LEMON-ANISE CREAM

3 cups assorted berries (blueberries, raspberries,
      strawberries,) washed and patted dry
1 cup whole milk ricotta cheese
½ cup mascarpone cheese
1 ½ tablespoons agave nectar
1 drop lemon essential oil
3 drops nutmeg essential oil
1 1/2 teaspoons ground anise seed
3 cups assorted berries (blueberries, raspberries,
      Strawberries,) washed and patted dry
½ tablespoon agave nectar
1 tablespoon fresh basil, chopped
1 tablespoon fresh mint, chopped

SERVES 4

In a blender or food processor, add the first 3 cups of assorted berries, ricotta cheese, mascarpone cheese, agave nectar, EO's and ground anise. Blend until smooth.

In a separate bowl, mix the next 3 cups of assorted berries, agave nectar and herbs.

Layer berries and the berry-cream either in a trifle dish or individual serving cups/glasses.

Serve cold.

continued

Berries with Lemon-Anise Cream (continued)

EO BENEFIT: Nutmeg EO may be helpful to ease nerve pain.

HINT: Serve with a scone, biscotti, or crispy cookie.

CARROT PUDDING (ala Gajar Halva)

1 ten ounce bag shredded carrots or 6 medium carrots,
        peeled and shredded
2 cups almond milk
1 cup coconut milk
½ cup packed brown sugar
1/4 cup golden raisins
2 tablespoons salted butter
¼ teaspoon ground cardamom
2 drops cinnamon essential oil
2 drops nutmeg essential oil
1 drop carrot seed essential oil
Dash salt
¼ cup roasted salted pistachio nuts,
2 tablespoons pistachio nuts, chopped

SERVES 4

In a medium sauce pan over medium high heat with the pan
covered, heat carrots and almond and coconut milks to a boil.
Reduce heat and simmer uncovered until the milk is absorbed
and mixture has a pudding like texture (about 45 minutes)

Stir in the remaining ingredients (except 2 tablespoons chopped
nuts).

Serve warm garnished with chopped pistachios.

continued

Carrot Pudding (continued)

EO BENEFIT: Carrot seed EO may be helpful for water retention.

HINT: The brown sugar can be replaced by 2 tablespoons of molasses.

OPTIONAL SERVING IDEA: This dessert isn't overly sweet and can be used as a side dish.

COCONUT ALMOND, KEY-LIME MACAROONS

Macaroons:
7 ounce bag of sweetened, shredded coconut
½ cup whole almonds, finely chopped
2 tablespoons fresh Key lime juice or concentrated
        Key lime juice (ex: Kermit's®)
2 drops lime essential oil
1 drop lemon essential oil
3 large egg whites, beaten to a froth
½ teaspoon vanilla
2 dashes cayenne

Frosting:
¾ cup white chocolate chips
1 teaspoon fresh Key lime juice or concentrated
        Key lime juice (ex: Kermit's®)
1 drop lime essential oil
2 tablespoons of milk, almond milk, coconut milk, or
        heavy cream

Garnish:
The zest from one medium sized lime or a Key lime

Preheat oven to 300 degrees. Line two large baking sheets with parchment paper.

continued

Make the cookies: Chop the almonds in a food processor. Combine all macaroon ingredients in a large bowl. Drop 1 tablespoon mounds of dough onto the prepared baking sheet about 2 inches apart. Cook until pale golden brown – about 18 to 20 minutes. Let rest for 5 minutes on the baking sheet, then move to a rack to cool completely.

Make the frosting: Add frosting ingredients to a microwaveable bowl. Cook on 50% power for 30 seconds, mix well – keep microwaving at 50% power in 30 second intervals, stirring in between, until smooth.
Use a spoon to drizzle the frosting atop each cooled macaroon. Garnish with the lime zest.

EO BENEFIT: Lime EO may encourage creativity.

HINT: If the frosting is a too thick to drizzle, add one tablespoon of tepid milk at a time until stirred to the right consistency.

BROWNIES

2 tablespoons unsalted butter
1 stick unsalted butter (1/2 cup)
½ cup unsweetened cocoa
2 large eggs
1 cup sugar
1/3 cup all purpose flour
1 teaspoon vanilla extract
¼ teaspoon salt
Essential oils (see below)

Preheat oven to 335 degrees.

Grease an 8 x 8 baking pan (metal or glass) with 2 tablespoons of butter.

Over low heat (or in the microwave at 60% power), melt the stick of butter; remove from heat and stir in the cocoa. Place this mixture into a large bowl and add the other ingredients one at a time in the order listed. Mix until blended.

Spread the mixture into the greased baking pan. Bake for 28 – 32 minutes.

Pick a type of brownie, and use these EO's.

PEPPERMINT BROWNIES – add 6 drops of peppermint EO

FALL FLAVORED BROWNIES – add 1 drop each clove, tangerine, cinnamon and nutmeg EO's

ORANGE BROWNIES – add 4 drops orange EO

ORANGE BARS

2 tablespoons unsalted better
1 cup cooked quinoa, cooled
1 cup walnut nuts, chopped
5 egg whites
Zest of 2 oranges
Juice of 2 oranges (about a 1/2 cup)
¾ cup sugar
1 stick of unsalted butter at room temperature
1/8 teaspoon salt
3 drops orange essential oil
1 drop basil essential oil

Preheat oven to 350 degrees. Use the 2 tablespoons of butter to grease the bottom and sides of an 8 x 8 baking pan.

In a bowl, mix all remaining ingredients and pour into the greased pan. Bake for 30 minutes.

EO BENEFIT: Orange EO may be helpful for relieving stress.

HINT: Use a food processor to chop the nuts.

CRÈME BRULEE WITH MAPLE-TANGERINE SYRUP

Custard:
6 egg yolks
4 tablespoons sugar
½ teaspoon vanilla extract
3 drops tarragon essential oil
2 drops coriander essential oil
2 ½ cups heavy cream

Syrup:
½ cup pure maple syrup at room temperature
8 drops tangerine essential oil

To caramelize the custard:
2 tablespoons white sugar
2 tablespoons brown sugar

Preheat oven to 320 degrees. Set 5 ramekins in a glass 9 x 13 casserole dish. Add water in the casserole dish until half way up the ramekin sides.

Beat egg yolks, sugar, vanilla, and custard listed EO's until creamy. Set aside.

Pour the cream into a saucepan over low heat. Heat until almost boiling, stirring often. Remove from heat. Using large spoon, put about ¼ cup of the cream into the egg yolk mixture - stir well - then add the egg mixture into the pan and beat until well combined.

continued

Crème Brulee with Maple-Tangerine Syrup (continued)

Put the pan back onto low heat, and continue to cook and stir for 3 - 5 minutes until the mixture thickens (it will coat the back of the spoon). Transfer the mixture into the 5 ramekin dishes.

Bake at 320 for 25 minutes or until set. Remove ramekins from the casserole dish let cool. Can be refrigerated overnight.

To serve:
Mix the maple syrup and tangerine EO together. Set aside.

Mix the sugars together and spoon and spread over the top of the custard. Use a kitchen torch or the broiler to melt and caramelize the sugars - be careful not to burn the sugar.

Spoon the syrup over the top of the brulees.

EO BENEFIT: Tarragon essential oil may be helpful to alleviate depression.

SPICE CAKE

2 tablespoons unsalted butter
2 cups sugar
1 cup butter, softened
4 eggs, lightly beaten
3 cups flour
1 teaspoon baking powder
1 teaspoon baking soda
1 cup buttermilk
2 drops cinnamon essential oil
2 drops clove essential oil
2 drops nutmeg essential oil

Preheat the oven to 350. Use the 2 tablespoons of butter to grease a 9 x 13 pan. If desired, lightly coat the greased pan with flour.

Cream sugar and butter together. Add beaten eggs and stir well (about 30 seconds).

In a separate bowl, mix dry ingredients.

Alternate adding some dry ingredients and some buttermilk into the sugar-butter mixture. Mixing in between until moistened. Add EO's and beat for 1 minute.

Pour cake mixture into pan. Bake for 35 - 40 minutes (until knife or toothpick comes out clean).

EO BENEFIT: Nutmeg EO may be helpful for fatigue.

HINT: Top with your favorite cream cheese frosting.

LAYERED APPLE BARS

½ cup unsalted butter
2 drops clove essential oil
2 drops nutmeg essential oil
2 drops cinnamon essential oil
1 ½ cups graham cracker crumbs
1 ½ cups caramel chips
2 cups dried apple, chopped
1 cup walnuts, chopped
¼ cup raisins
1 14 ounce can sweetened condensed milk
1 1/3 cups shredded coconut

Preheat oven to 350 degrees.

Place butter in 9 x 13 pan and put into oven to melt the butter. Remove the pan from the oven and add the EO's, stir well. Evenly spread the graham cracker crumbs over the butter mixture.

Next, evenly spread the caramel chips over the crumbs, follow with the walnuts and raisins.

Evenly pour the sweetened condensed milk over the walnuts and raisins. Top with shredded coconut.

Bake 25 - 30 minutes until edges and top are golden brown. Cool and slice into bars.

EO BENEFIT: Clove EO may be helpful as an antioxidant.

HINT: Delicious served with a scoop of cinnamon or vanilla ice cream.

LEMON-BASIL BLUEBERRY UPSIDE DOWN CAKE

1 tablespoon butter, softened
1/2 tablespoon olive oil
1 pint fresh blueberries, rinsed and patted dry
1/4 cup sugar
2 drops lemon essential oil
1 ¾ cup all purpose flour
1 teaspoon baking powder
½ teaspoon baking soda
½ teaspoon salt
1 stick unsalted butter at room temperature
3/4 cup sugar
1/4 cup light brown sugar
2 large eggs at room temperature
4 drops lemon essential oil
2 drops basil essential oil
1 teaspoon vanilla extract
¾ cup whole milk
¼ cup plain Greek yogurt
2 tablespoons fresh basil, chopped for garnish (optional)

Preheat oven to 350 degrees. Use the tablespoon of butter and olive oil to grease an 8" or 9" round cake pan.

Gently mix blueberries, sugar, and lemon essential oil in a small bowl. Pour into the prepared cake pan.

In a bowl, whisk flour, baking powder, baking soda and salt together. Set aside.

continued

In another bowl, use an electric mixer to beat the butter, sugar, and brown sugar together until fluffy and sugar is mostly dissolved (about 8 minutes). While still blending, add the eggs one at a time, then add the essential oils and extracts until blended.

Add half the flour mixture, blend; add the milk and Greek yogurt, blend; add the other half of the flour mixture, blend. Pour this mixture over the berries.

Cook 45 minutes or until an inserted toothpick comes out clean of cake batter. Run a knife or small spatula around the inside of the pan to release the cake from the sides. Let cake sit for at least 15 minutes, then invert onto a serving plate.

EO BENEFIT: Basil EO may be helpful as a mood enhancer.

PEACH-BERRY COBBLER

2 tablespoons butter

For the filling:
9 medium or 7 large peaches, pitted and sliced
½ pint blueberries, rinsed and patted dry
Juice of 1 lemon
2 drops cinnamon essential oil
2 drops clove essential oil
2 drops nutmeg essential oils

For the topping:
1 16 ounce can B&M® Brown Bread with Raisins, cubed
½ cup light brown sugar, loosely packed
2 drops cinnamon essential oil
½ cup chopped walnuts
¼ cup butter cut into 1 inch pieces

Preheat oven to 350. Use the 2 tablespoons of butter to grease the bottom and sides of a 9 x 13 glass baking dish.

Gently mix the peaches, blueberries, lemon juice, and essential oils. Place in the greased pan.

Make the topping: In a bowl, crumble the bread and mix with brown sugar, walnuts, and essential oil. Evenly spread the mixture atop the fruit mixture. Dot with the cubes of butter.

Bake uncovered for 40 minutes. Watch so that the bread topping doesn't burn (cover with foil if necessary).

BANANA-LIME QUINOA PUDDING

1 ½ cups purified water
¾ cup quinoa, rinsed & drained
3 medium sized very ripe bananas
2 tablespoons sugar
Dash of salt
1 ½ cups whole milk
1 tablespoon butter, melted
2 egg yolks
½ teaspoon vanilla extract
4 drops lime essential oil
1 tablespoon lime zest

Over high heat, bring water and quinoa to a boil. Stir, then reduce heat to simmer until quinoa is cooked – about 15 minutes.

In a bowl, mash bananas, sugar, and salt. Add the milk; stir well. Add this mixture to the quinoa pan. Cook for 10 minutes on medium-low to low heat.

Put the egg yolks in a small bowl, add 2 tablespoons of hot banana-milk mixture and stir well, then add all of the yolk mixture into the pan. Cook and stir until pudding is thickened.

Remove pan from heat and cool 2 minutes. Mix in melted butter, vanilla extract, EO, and zest.

Serve warm or cold.

continued

Banana-Lime Quinoa Pudding (continued)

EO BENEFIT: Lime EO may be helpful to boost the immune system.

HINT: Adding some of the egg mixture into the egg yolks first, rather than putting the yolks directly into the pan, helps to temper the heat level so that the eggs do not turn to scrambled eggs when added into the pudding.

CHOCOLATE-MOCHA CINNAMON CHEESECAKE

2 tablespoons unsalted butter

Crust:
1 ½ cups crushed ginger snap cookies, processed or crushed into crumbs (ex: Pepperidge Farm® Gingerman™)
¼ cup butter, melted

Cheesecake filling:
16 ounces cream cheese
1 cup sugar
3 tablespoons instant espresso crystals, dissolved
        in 3 tablespoons hot water, cooled
1 teaspoon vanilla extract
4 drops cinnamon essential oil
2 large eggs, lightly beaten
1 cup semi-chocolate chips, melted

For the whipped cream:
1 cup heavy cream / whipping cream
2 drops orange essential oil

Use the 2 tablespoons of butter to grease the sides of a 9" spring form pan. Preheat oven to 350 degrees.

continued

Chocolate-Mocha Cinnamon Cheesecake (continued)

Mix cookie crumbs with melted butter. Firmly press into the bottom and slightly up the sides of the greased pan. Set aside.

With a mixer, blend together cream cheese, sugar, espresso, vanilla, and cinnamon essential oil until smooth. Add the eggs and mix on low speed until combined.

Gently fold in the melted chocolate until combined. Pour the mixture over the cookie crumbs; smooth the top with a knife or spatula.

Bake for 45 - 50 minutes until the center is almost set and sides of cake have pulled away from the edge of the pan.

Remove from oven, run a knife around the inner rim of the pan to loosen the cake, and set aside to cool. Once cool, remove the outer rim of the springform pan and refrigerate the cheesecake for 4 hours or overnight.

Make the whipped cream just before serving. Add the cream and orange EO to a bowl and beat on high until peaks form. Do not overbeat into butter. Serve spooned atop slices of the cheesecake.

continued

Chocolate-Mocha Cinnamon Cheesecake (continued)

EO BENEFIT: Cinnamon EO may help to stimulate the immune system.

HINT: To make the whipped cream, put metal or glass bowl and beaters into the freezer at least 20 minutes before using to make whipped cream.

INDEX

Lime: 21, 31, 50, 56, 65, 69, 71, 73, 75, 98, 100, 117, 123, 149, 163, 174
Nutmeg: 71, 143, 159, 161, 165, 169, 170, 173
Orange: 9, 33, 39, 57, 165, 166, 176
Oregano: 13, 18, 42, 59, 67, 76, 84, 93, 95, 96, 99, 102, 106, 115, 121, 131
Peppermint: 165
Rosemary: 36, 82, 90, 94, 133, 155
Tangerine: 46, 65, 123, 165, 167
Tarragon: 146, 167
Thyme: 76, 88, 90, 129, 145, 148, 153, 155

Fish: 19, 28, 44, 49, 86, 100, 113, 123, 126

Lamb: 121

Pork: 11, 18, 50, 52, 73, 80, 104, 106, 117, 133, 151

Shrimp: 9, 29, 57, 71, 82, 111, 131

Turkey: 13, 15, 69, 93

Vegetarian (fruits, vegetables, and/or dairy): 16, 21, 22, 24, 41, 42, 45, 46, 48, 54, 55, 65, 67, 75, 90, 94, 96, 99, 103, 129, 134, 135, 139, 140, 141, 142, 143, 144, 145, 146, 147, 148, 150, 152, 153, 155, 159, 161, 163, 165, 166, 167, 169, 170, 171, 173, 174, 176

Made in the USA
Middletown, DE
08 October 2020